The Ultimate Weaning & Toddler Cookbook

Charlotte Stirling-Reed

Bestselling author of *How to Wean Your Baby*

The Ultimate Weaning & Toddler Cookbook

Contents

Introduction

As a Baby & Child Nutritionist, I have spoken with thousands of families and know how tricky feeding little ones can be. As a busy mum of two, I also know how hectic family life can be and am passionate about helping families make mealtimes happy occasions for all.

I'm so excited to be writing this book for you. So many of you have been in touch saying how much you have enjoyed my recipes over the years and I'm always asked for more … so here are 100 brand-new delicious recipes for you and your family to enjoy. My aim with this book is for it to be an extension of *How to Wean Your Baby* and *How to Feed Your Toddler*, giving you more ideas and inspiration to help you think outside the box and continue to offer a variety of tasty foods to your little ones from weaning and beyond.

Whereas *How to Wean Your Baby* contains all the details about how, when, why and what to do when you start weaning, and *How to Feed Your Toddler* helps you shape your children's food preferences and deal with any of the trials and tribulations that go hand-in-hand with feeding toddlers, this book offers tips and helpful advice for these ages, but focuses much more on the recipes.

For those of you new to my books, I really hope this baby and toddler cookbook will give you not only the knowledge to feed your little ones with confidence, but also lots of inspiration and new meal ideas so that mealtimes become an enjoyable experience for the whole family!

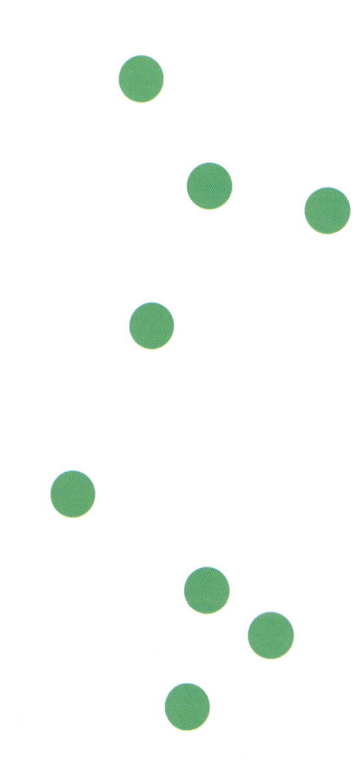

 # How to Use This Book

The first part of this book is a very general guide to weaning and feeding toddlers. It covers the basics and the need-to-knows so that you can confidently and safely start your baby on solid foods, including how to recognise when they are ready for solids, which foods to start with and how to help your baby move on to more complex meals and textures over time.

The second – and much bigger – part of this book offers a real range of family-friendly recipes, designed for busy parents/carers and carefully balanced with your little ones in mind. For those of you who want to, we start with some simple mashes and purees, before moving on to more elaborate 'bridge meals', which aim to move your baby from mashes to more complex dishes that emulate the kinds of meals we might be eating ourselves. Finally, the book introduces meals that your baby can have alongside the rest of the family. This includes lots of ideas for finger foods, as well as breakfasts, lunches, dinners, snacks and celebration foods. I hope you and your little one love these recipes, which are all designed to give them the best start in their journey with food.

What is Weaning?

Weaning is the process of gradually moving your baby from a milk-only diet to a more complex diet that eventually looks similar to what we eat as adults. It's a gentle and gradual process that should ideally be led by your baby and continued at their own pace.

What can I Expect?

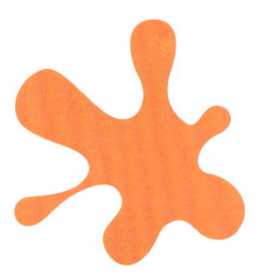

- Weaning is different for every baby. Some love it right away, while others take a little while to adjust to solid foods.

- Babies all have different appetites. If your little one doesn't eat much – especially early on – that's perfectly normal.

- Babies need to learn *how* to eat – this takes time and needs practice, skill-building and experimentation.

- A big part of babies learning *how* to eat comes from watching *you* eat yourself, so try to eat with them as much as possible.

- Babies make plenty of faces when trying new foods. This doesn't mean they 'don't like' certain foods, more that they are surprised, shocked or unsure at this new experience.

- It can take multiple attempts before some foods are accepted, so don't give up with any that are initially rejected. Babies like what they are familiar with.

- Making a mess is all part of weaning. Food on the floor, in their hair and over their face is helping them to learn, as well as getting them even more familiar with new tastes and flavours.

- Parent/carer confidence can make a massive difference in helping the journey to go smoothly. So, try to prep a little ahead to ensure it's more enjoyable for you both. If you need a little more guidance, *How to Wean Your Baby* is a step-by-step plan that will fully equip and empower you to take this exciting next step.

When Should I Start Weaning?

Generally, in the UK, it's recommended to begin offering your baby solid foods at *around* six months of age, but, more importantly, look out for the following signs of readiness:

1   A baby can sit up with minimal support and hold their own head and neck steady.

2   A baby can explore hand–eye coordination and so can see food, pick it up and bring it towards their mouth by themselves.

3   A baby will have less of a tongue thrust reflex and be able to swallow food when it's eventually offered (see box below).

Once you see these happening together and regularly, it's safe to say your baby is likely to be ready for solid foods. However, always speak to your health visitor if you think your baby is ready to be weaned earlier than *around* six months.

What is the tongue thrust reflex?

This is where a baby's tongue responds in a reflex manner and moves forward in response to touch, protruding out of their mouth. As a baby moves towards six months, this reflex should reduce (but often won't completely disappear by six months), thereby making it easier for them to swallow food and not push it all back out with their tongue.

Baby-Led Weaning Versus Spoon-Feeding

Baby-led weaning is simply where you offer your baby pieces of soft solid foods and let them self-feed right from the start. Spoon-feeding is where you largely offer more mashed or pureed foods from a spoon to begin with. Ultimately, you don't have to decide between the two and follow just one method of feeding your baby. The truth is that the combined approach can actually be best for you and your baby's confidence, and also for developing their eating skills at the start of weaning. I'm a fan of offering babies *some* mashes from a spoon, alongside finger foods at mealtimes right from the start of weaning.

As your baby gets more experienced with the textures you're offering, you can gradually offer more challenging textures at mealtimes and follow their lead with how well they are accepting them over time (see pages 16–17 for more guidance on introducing different textures).

> ✳ **Remember:** Babies don't need teeth for weaning; their gums are solid and can easily break down soft foods.

What Foods Should I Start Weaning With?

I'm a big advocate of starting weaning with 'veg-led weaning', which I guide you through step-by-step in my first book, *How to Wean Your Baby*. When you start by offering your baby tastes of single veggies, it helps them to explore more varied flavours (not just sweet ones) for their first tastes of food. Research has also shown that it helps increase their acceptance of veggies and a variety of tastes later on.

Some veggies that can be great options as first foods include:

- broccoli
- cauliflower
- potato
- green beans
- asparagus
- avocado (although not a vegetable, it has a neutral flavour)
- spinach
- kale
- swede

To make veggies into purees:

For most veggies, simply chop them into finger/stick shapes, where possible.

Boil or steam until they are super soft and squidge nicely between your finger and thumb.

Ideally offer your baby a different vegetable each day for the first week or so of weaning before moving on to other foods such as proteins, carbohydrates and a variety of vegetables and fruits (see page 20 for more on this).

For avocado, simply peel and destone and mash the flesh into the desired texture.

→ Drain and either blend or mash (depending on the texture you prefer to start with).

→ Once cool, offer this alongside a few sticks of whole super soft finger food pieces for your baby's first meals.

You might want to add a little of the vegetable cooking water or some of baby's usual milk to the purees or mashes to loosen them (see page 44 for more on mashes and purees).

✳ Most veggies can also be offered as finger foods (if they don't work as finger foods, for example, spinach, use another vegetable, such as a broccoli floret or a potato stick, to dip into a spinach puree or mash).

**Offer soft finger foods
to help with texture
exploration**

**Move to 'mashed' foods
by adding less liquid and
blending less**

If you're offering purees (you'll see some examples on pages 45–53), it's good to be mindful that babies need to progress through textures *fairly* quickly as we know from research that it's important for babies to experience soft lumps and different textures in their food before around nine months of age.

After a little while, start to mash with a fork and allow for plenty of lumps

Go at baby's pace, but aim to move through textures nice and early!

Move through textures gradually by adding less fluid, blending less and moving to more mashed and lumpy options.

Finger Foods

It's important to offer finger foods to your baby, even if at the start you're a little nervous of this (which is perfectly normal), as finger foods help your baby to really develop those skills needed for eating, such as biting, chewing and swallowing, using their oral motor muscles and self-feeding. If you don't start offering finger foods at the very start of weaning, that's OK, but ideally they need to be introduced during the first few weeks of weaning.

Many veggies, including super soft broccoli florets, potato and ripe avocado, make fantastic early finger food options and, after a while of trying these, you can offer much more variety, such as soft-cooked salmon, soft pasta shapes and lightly toasted bread, to help your baby explore more. Once they've gained a little experience with finger foods, you can start to introduce more variety, such as the finger food recipes on pages 75–107. Most of these are perfectly fine for your baby from the start of their weaning journey (unless otherwise noted), but it's good to experiment with a few options first for your baby to get the hang of self-feeding. Just make sure that any finger food you offer at the start is easy to squidge between your finger and thumb, so you know it's soft enough for your baby to manage.

Some of my favourite first finger foods and next-step finger foods include:

- broccoli
- avocado
- potato
- swede
- cauliflower

Then:

- fusilli pasta
- salmon
- soft-cooked chicken
- egg yolks
- banana
- soft pears

How Many Meals a Day Should I Offer?

It's best to start with just one meal a day to allow your baby to get used to this new food and the process of eating … and go at their pace as much as possible. If your baby is enjoying weaning and eating some food at mealtimes, you might want to move up to another meal after a week or so (there is a handy checklist for this in *How to Wean Your Baby*). If your baby seems less sure and is not eating much or doesn't want to be in the highchair for too long, be a little more patient and perhaps move from one to two to three meals a little more slowly.

It's important that foods don't hugely displace milk – especially early on during weaning – but you do want your little one to enjoy and be happy to explore foods (see below for more on how much milk to offer during weaning).

What Do I Do About Milk?

At the very start of weaning, babies will still have a similar amount of milk each day to before they started weaning. This is because weaning is not about swapping calories from milk to calories from foods – just yet! Instead, it is about gradually helping your baby develop the skills needed to eat and learn to accept a wide variety of flavours and textures in their diet. Milk is still a key player and is where your baby will get most of their nutrition and calories from until at least 10–12 months of age, when food starts to somewhat take over. Check out my meal plan examples on pages 32–3 for some simple ideas of what the day's structure *might* look like.

As a very general guideline, the NHS in the UK recommends that formula-fed babies are offered around 600ml of milk in 24 hours from around 7 months of age and around 400ml of milk in 24 hours at around 10 months of age.

For breastfed babies, it's recommended to offer milk responsively (as and when your baby indicates they need it). However, it can be a good idea to try to bring a 'mealtime routine' into play when weaning begins, so that your little one starts to become familiar with when to expect solids versus breast milk as this can help with their acceptance of solid foods (see pages 32–3 for some example plans).

Next Steps After First Tastes

Variety is so key early on in your little one's weaning journey to help them accept and become familiar with a variety of foods. I go into a lot more detail on this in *How to Wean Your Baby*, but on pages 45–53, there are some simple mashes/purees which start to include some more adventurous tastes and flavours than the single veggies I suggested on page 13, including some herbs and spices.

Your baby can then move on to the 'bridge meals' on pages 57–71, which will start to reflect the kind of meals you might eat as a family. You can always continue to blend or mash foods as you see fit to help get the texture right for your baby.

After single tastes of veggies, the meals you offer might gradually look like this over the next days and weeks of weaning:

1.

VEG **+** PROTEIN

| e.g. | broccoli | + | lentils/beef mince |
| or | avocado | + | butter beans |

2.

VEG **+** PROTEIN **+** CARB

| e.g. | carrot | + | chickpeas | + | mashed rice |
| or | spinach | + | cod | + | pasta |

3.

VEG/ FRUIT **+** PROTEIN **+** CARB **+** A FLAVOUR

| e.g. | courgette | + | chicken | + | potato sticks | + | squeeze of lemon |

It's all about gradually moving your baby on to meals that work for the whole family as soon as you can.

Fruit

You can add fruits whenever you like, but try not to focus only on sweeter flavours during weaning and beyond, as little ones like what they are used to and are born to prefer sweeter tastes. Offering largely sweeter foods can make it trickier for them to accept more savoury tastes as alternatives.

Foods to Avoid

There are some foods you need to avoid offering to your baby during weaning. There isn't really a cut-off as to when you can offer most of these (with the exception of honey, which can be offered from one year of age, though it is still an added sugar so isn't advised even after this). It's best to wait until your baby has developed their immune system, has really good eating skills and also has explored a wide variety of foods and developed a positive pattern of eating – which can take a few years. Largely it's recommended not to offer salt/sugar/choking risk foods and the other foods in this list until your baby is around four to five years of age.

Foods to avoid include:

- salt and salty foods: little ones don't need added salt in their diet

- sugar and foods with added sugar: little ones also don't need added sugar in their diet

- honey: can contain bacteria that is dangerous for babies under one

- unpasteurised dairy: can contain listeria that could be dangerous for small children with less well-developed immune systems

- raw fish, raw meat and raw shellfish: in case of any food poisoning, which is more of a risk for little ones with less well-developed immune systems

- shark, swordfish and marlin: as they can contain high levels of mercury

- rice milk: as it can contain small amounts of arsenic

- choking risk foods (see opposite)

quartered

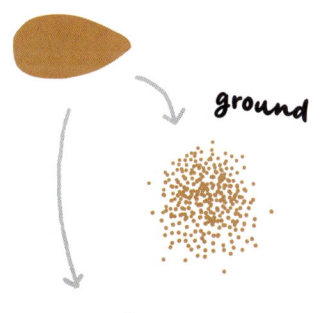

ground

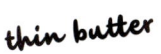

thin butter

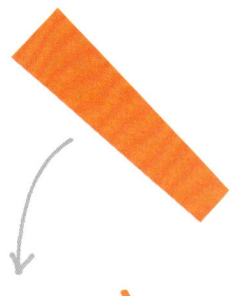

grated

Foods that are higher risks for choking for babies include:

- whole grapes
- whole nuts and large seeds
- large, round foods like cherry tomatoes, blueberries and olives
- thick dollops of peanut butter
- hard sticks of foods like raw carrot sticks, chunks of cheese and apple and sausages
- some dried fruits, such as large dates, large whole raisins or sticky sultanas

These foods need to be avoided or adapted by crushing, cooking, mashing, grating, quartering, blending or thinning. For example, large beans and peas can be a choking hazard for babies, but it depends how they are served and also on the eating skills and experience of the baby. It's best to flatten or squash beans and peas for babies initially until they are older and have developed excellent oral motor skills for eating a variety of foods. As your baby builds their eating skills, they will get more efficient at eating and be able to eat these foods in some forms, but they will need gradual practice.

In the recipes, I've added notes where some foods, such as beans, tomatoes or dried fruits, might need adapting for smaller children and babies. If you're ever unsure, it's always best to mash foods or adapt them slightly to make them less of a risk.

 To reduce the risk of choking:

- Ensure your baby is developmentally ready and showing all the key signs of readiness (see page 11).

- Always sit with your baby when they are eating.

- Ensure they are sitting down and sitting upright properly for every meal, not lying back or reclined at all.

- Offer a variety, following their lead with textures as they develop their eating skills.

- Role-model how to eat effectively by eating with them as much as you can.

- Offer safe foods: remove any pips, stringy bits, tough skins, large fatty bits of meat, hard parts or large round foods (including any of the choking hazards above), and any other parts of foods that are harder for babies to swallow.

How to Introduce Food Allergens

In *How to Wean your Baby*, there is a step-by-step guide to introducing food allergens. You can also find out more information on my website **www.srnutrition.co.uk**.

Advice around allergens has changed in recent years. We now know that early introduction of allergens may be protective and help reduce the risk of an allergy developing later on. The current advice is therefore that allergens should be introduced to babies at the start of weaning alongside meals (I usually say to offer them *after* you've introduced your baby to their first tastes of single veggies – say, after a week or so of weaning).

When you offer allergens, it's important to ensure that you offer them:

- one at a time (so only offer one of the common allergens within one day – you might want to leave a gap of two to three days before trying another allergen food)

- in tiny amounts – ideally an amount equivalent to the tip of a teaspoon (perhaps mixed in a puree or a mash), so you are only exposing them to a really small amount of an allergen on the first go

- as the only new food that day – so only offer an allergen alongside foods that your baby has already tried before e.g. if you've never offered your baby lentils, don't offer your baby a common allergen alongside lentils for the very first time

- ideally early on in the day so you can spend plenty of time with your baby observing any reactions that might occur

This advice is also relevant for any recipes in this book that contain allergens. (I've highlighted any recipes where allergens are included.) For example, if a recipe calls for peanut butter alongside other foods your baby hasn't had before, it's best to first introduce a small amount of the allergen food on its own or with foods your baby has already had before. Once your baby has tried the allergen food with no reaction once or twice, you can start exploring the full recipe including the allergen food.

It's important to remember that *most* babies won't be allergic to foods (only around 5–8 per cent of two-year-olds have diagnosed food allergies) and there is a difference between an allergy and a contact reaction (an irritation to the skin where food has touched).

Is my baby's rash a food allergy or contact reaction?

Probable contact reaction

* The redness/rash should be localised to the mouth, lips, chin and face where the food has touched. If your little one has been self-feeding it can also appear on the hands and wrists.

* The area affected is likely to look red and angry.

* The redness should start to subside by itself, without using any medication.

* Your little one should generally be unfazed by the reaction. They may be a little grizzly if the meal has been removed from them.

* Foods rich in histamine such as spinach and aubergine may cause your little one to have a contact reaction.

Could be an allergy

* The redness progresses to other areas of the body such as the legs, tummy, back.

* There are widespread hives (a raised red rash).

* Once the food has been removed and the baby cleaned the reaction progresses further. By this I mean further symptoms appear such as a wheeze or vomiting.

* Your little one appears distressed by the reaction or becomes floppy or sleepy.

* Your little one is itchy elsewhere on the body such as the back, legs etc. They may however be itchy if they have eczema, but you will know what your little one's normal behaviour is.

---

* **If your baby has any severe symptoms dial 999 immediately for help.** For mild to moderate symptoms, call 111 for advice. Avoid the food and speak to your GP to discuss getting a referral to an allergy team.

For more advice, contact Allergy UK or the British Society for Allergy & Clinical Immunology (see Resources, page 217).

The most common allergens in the UK include:

* dairy foods
* eggs
* fish and shellfish
* peanuts
* sesame
* soy
* tree nuts
* wheat

Immediate reactions your baby may have:

← Severe symptoms, such as swollen tongue, persistent cough, hoarse cry, difficulty or noisy breathing or going pale and floppy or unconscious/unresponsive.

← Mild to moderate symptoms, such as swollen lips and face or eyes, itchy skin rash e.g. hives, abdominal pain or vomiting.

Moving On With Solids

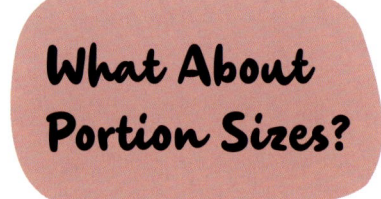

The recipes in this book will help you to transition through meals, from the single tastes shown on page 13, to the mashes and puree examples shown on pages 45–53, to the bridge meals on pages 57–71 and eventually to proper family meals.

By the time your baby is around 9–10 months of age they will ideally easily be on three meals a day and may start having a little less in the way of milk. Ideally, they will have moved through textures (see pages 16–17) and be starting to eat more complex meals (no longer on mashes or purees) and developing eating skills, practising self-feeding and also eating a really wide variety of foods. Babies can eat most things by now (aside from the foods listed on page 22) and many of the choking hazard foods can be adapted to make them safe for babies to eat once they are experienced with a variety of textures.

Once your baby is 12 months old, they should ideally be having similar meals and textures to the rest of the family and joining in regularly with family mealtimes. You might still need to adapt some textures for toddlers and that's OK. Their calories will largely come from their solid foods now, with fewer coming from milk.

What About Portion Sizes?

All babies are likely to be different, which is why there are no portion size guides for babies – some babies eat a fair amount and have larger appetites, while others are more reserved in their portions and are full after a smaller amount of food.

Your baby is the best predictor of their own appetite, so, rather than focusing on what portions they 'should' be eating, try to look out for signs that they are full up, such as:

- pushing food away
- clamping mouth shut
- turning their head away from the food
- crying during the meal
- trying to get down from the table

If your little one shows any of these signs, they may be indicating that they don't want food and so it might be best to end the meal. They might be full, or tired, or many other things, but it's important to follow their cues and not keep them in the highchair when they don't want to be there as this may have an impact on their feelings around mealtimes in the future.

Always avoid forcing or pressuring a baby to eat any foods.

Balancing Baby and Toddler Meals

Once your baby is eating more substantial meals, and especially when they are having three meals a day, it's important to make sure that they are getting plenty of 'balance' at each mealtime. This helps to ensure that they are getting all the energy and nutrients they need, but also that they become really familiar with eating all the foods that make up a balanced diet.

Babies and toddlers (as well as adults) need the following food groups every day and at most meals (and when they are over one, possibly in snacks too) to help ensure that they get all the energy and nutrients they need to grow and develop and be healthy:

Starchy foods: Wholegrains provide fibre as well as plenty of energy and B vitamins. Babies and toddlers shouldn't exclusively eat wholegrain/brown varieties, as too many high-fibre foods may bulk out little tummies and leave less room for other varied foods, so white varieties are fine for babies and toddlers too. It's good to offer starchy foods at most meals and with snacks, if offered.

Protein/iron: Proteins are the building blocks for growth that support many functions in the body. Protein- and iron-rich foods are often similar and include foods such as lentils, beans, pulses, fish, meat and eggs. These contain nutrients that are essential for growing children, as they play a role in delivering oxygen to our body's cells and are essential for brain development too. Many children don't get enough iron in their diet and it's a really important one to offer at most mealtimes for growing babies and toddlers.

Vegetables and fruits: These offer fibre, hydration and a wide variety of vitamins, minerals and phytonutrients, which are essential for immunity, muscle health, nervous system and many other factors that help keep our little ones healthy. Aim for five mini portions of these a day from around the age of one (think of the palm of your child's hand as a rough portion).

Dairy foods: These contain calcium for growing bones (as well as plenty of other nutrients). Children under one will get most of their calcium from breast or formula milk, but a little dairy or fortified alternatives can be added to their foods. For children over one, it's important to include dairy foods and/or fortified alternatives around three times a day. It's recommended to have around 350–400ml of milk a day from 12 months of age, or around three portions of dairy. These can be offered as breast milk feeds and/or as milk, yoghurt and cheese (or fortified alternatives) spread throughout the day as desired. For children over one, if you're still breastfeeding a few times a day, this will cover most of your baby's calcium needs (as well as still providing various other benefits to your baby), but you might want to include a portion or two of dairy or fortified alternatives as this helps to add other nutrients in their diet and get your little one used to these foods too.

Ideally, we want to start building this balance in from early on in weaning (see page 21) as these food groups all provide important elements to our little one's diet to help them grow and develop properly.

How much water does my baby need?

Babies get most of their fluid needs from their usual milk and the foods they are eating during weaning. However, water can be offered in small amounts at the start of weaning. A few sips in an open cup are best to help babies learn how to start drinking as we do as adults.

Sips of water with meals are enough from around six months of age and water doesn't need to be boiled first once baby is six months – straight from the tap is fine. After 12 months, little ones might start to need more in the way of fluids (especially as they are often having less fluids from milk at this stage) so, as a very general rule of thumb, it's recommended to offer:

- 3–4 cups at 1–2 years*
- 4–5 cups at 2–3 years*   (*A cup is around 200ml.)

Key Vitamins and Minerals for Babies and Toddlers

Some key vitamins and minerals for babies and toddlers include:

Iron: needed for many functions and often lacking in young children's diets. Found in lentils, meats, egg yolks, nuts and seeds.

Calcium: essential for healthy bone growth. Good sources include dairy foods, nuts and seeds, dark green leafy veggies and fortified foods such as bread and alternative milks.

Iodine: important for brain function, largely found in dairy foods and fish and sometimes in fortified milks. If these foods aren't consumed, you may need to consider a supplement.

 **Vitamin A:** important for eye health and can be low in some children's diets. A supplement is recommended by the UK government. Good sources include orange and red veggies and fruits and meat and eggs.

 **Vitamin D:** very hard to get from foods alone and is important in helping the body to absorb calcium for healthy bones. Supplements with 8.5–10mcg of vitamin D are recommended for babies from birth OR from when they are having less than 500ml of formula milk (as it's already added in the formula) until they are five years of age, when they may only need supplements for vitamin D in the winter months.

 Vitamin C: a possible supplement is recommended for vitamin C, but it's actually fairly easy for your baby or toddler to get enough vitamin C if they are eating plenty of (and a variety of) fruits and vegetables. Vitamin C is important for supporting the immune system and is found in citrus fruits and more generally in fruit and vegetables.

For babies who are on restricted diets, have multiple allergies, aren't eating a balanced diet or have any particular feeding issues, they may need extra supplementation, but it's likely to be on a case-by-case basis so make sure you see a healthcare professional for more support.

Vegan weaning

You can absolutely offer your baby a vegan or vegetarian diet during weaning, but you will need to ensure you're offering a really good balance of all the food groups, and there might be some nutrients that you need to be aware of to ensure your baby is getting enough. For example, omega-3, iodine and vitamin B12 are all a lot more challenging to obtain on a vegan diet and vegetarians might need to ensure their baby/toddler is having enough iron and omega-3 fatty acids too. Speak to a healthcare professional if you're unsure and or are thinking of weaning your child on a vegan diet.

Dealing with Food Refusal

Food refusal and fussy eating is often par for the course when raising kids, and especially toddlers! *How to Feed Your Toddler* has a whole section on coping with fussy eating, but here are some of my favourite tips for handling food refusal. I have lots more resources to help with this on my website too, so do check that out.

- **Don't sweat it**: know that food refusal happens and it's OK. The more we are nonchalant about it, the less likely it might be to become a 'thing'.

- **Expect appetite variations**: babies' and toddlers' appetites are affected by so much, including the weather, illness, teething and reaching certain milestones.

- **Eat together as much as you can**: role-modelling makes a big difference, so, right from the start, try to have meals together and eat similar (if not the same) foods as your little ones. This is why I've included 'bridge meals' on page 54 to help this start to take shape early on.

- **Avoid overly drawing attention to food refusal** and especially don't label your child a 'fussy eater' as this will likely exacerbate the situation.

- **Find ways to make mealtimes calm and enjoyable**: making them a place your kids *want* to be is so key to helping reduce food refusal in time.

- **Take the pressure off**: although it's super tempting to tell your little ones to 'eat up' or gently force a spoon into their mouth – or even bribe them to eat something on their plate – research shows that this doesn't work and actually backfires. Keep the pressure to a minimum at mealtimes to help improve eating in the long run.

- **Avoid alternatives**: offering a second or third option if the first meal is refused might be helpful in filling them up in the short term, but if it becomes a regular and 'normal' thing around the table, you might find that the number of acceptable meals gets smaller and smaller over time. Ideally have a plan for your meals and stick to it. You can offer extras as sides and also give your little one a choice of A or B to help with their independence.

- **Allow mealtime autonomy**: you're in charge of what's on offer, but let them decide how much they eat. They are the dictators of their own appetite, not us.

- **Remember that children like what they are familiar with**: offering something new is unlikely to be gobbled up right away in most households (including mine) so offer new meals and foods with familiar items – for example, offer a new curry with familiar foods such as a side of smashed peas, some rice and a few dollops of yoghurt.

 Mealtime tips

Below are some tips for helping to make mealtimes more enjoyable for the whole family:

- Try to have regular family mealtimes where adults and children sit together.

- Make it fun and/or at the very least a time for calm.

- Let them get down if they are unhappy or say they've had enough.

- Ensure they are sitting comfortably as this can affect their willingness to stay.

- Offer *some* independence around some food choices and let them explore meals and food at their own pace.

- Avoid pressure or coaxing or forcing them to eat and try to avoid bringing any anxieties or frustrations to the mealtime table.

- Try buffet meals where there are sides and plenty of foods on display.

- Avoid focusing on food refusal too much and use the phrase 'That's OK, you don't have to eat it' where needed.

Meal Plan Examples

These are very generalised examples of the food and milk plan your baby *might* have at different ages. Of course, every baby is so different, so there really isn't a one-size-fits-all routine and you might find that your baby's schedule is very different to the ones below, which is OK. I just wanted to give some very loose examples to give an idea of what might be a typical structure. Pick times that fit into your own family's routine, but try to stick to a regular structure when offering solids and when feeding your toddler.

Six to Seven Months

Morning	Baby's usual milk on waking
Breakfast	Puree/mash + finger food (optional)
Nap	Offer baby's usual milk before/after their nap
Lunch	Savoury puree/mash + finger food
Nap	Offer baby's usual milk before/after their nap
Dinner	–
Before Bed	Baby's usual milk before bedtime

Your baby may still have their usual milk feeds during the night and also may have extra milk feeds during the day.

Seven to Nine Months

Morning	Baby's usual milk on waking
Breakfast	Mashes/porridge/cereal/muffins/pancakes +/or veggie/fruit fingers (be sure to leave a gap after morning milk)
Nap	Offer baby's usual milk before/after their nap
Lunch	Meal with veg, protein + carbohydrate, including finger foods
Nap	Offer baby's usual milk before/after their nap
Dinner	Balanced family-style meals, adapted + including finger foods
Before Bed	Baby's usual milk before bedtime

Your baby may still have their usual milk feeds during the night and also may have extra milk feeds during the day.

Ten to Twelve Months

Around this time, your baby might start to want breakfast first in the morning, so you can reduce or cut out the first milk of the day and opt for brekkie first. All babies are different.

Your baby may still have milk feeds during the night; just keep a check on whether this might be affecting their appetite for solid foods during the day.

Morning	Baby's usual milk on waking (optional)
Breakfast	Porridge/cereal/muffins/pancakes etc., including finger foods
Nap	Offer baby's usual milk before/after their nap
Lunch	Balanced family-style meal with veg, protein + carbohydrate, including finger foods
Nap	Offer baby's usual milk before/after their nap
Dinner	Balanced family-style meals, adapted + including finger foods
Before Bed	Baby's usual milk before bedtime

Twelve+ Months

Your child *may* need two healthy snacks in between meals from 12 months of age. This varies from child to child and is a way of topping up energy and nutrient intakes. Breast milk, cow's milk or fortified plant milks can be included as part of snacks.

Your child may still have extra breast milk/their usual milk through the day, which is perfectly fine – just be sure the milk isn't filling them up and displacing other foods.

Breakfast	Family-style breakfast e.g. porridge, cereal, toast or pancakes
Snack	Balanced snack (if required)
Lunch	Balanced family-style meal with veg, protein + carbohydrates, possibly adapted
Snack	Balanced snack (if required)
Dinner	Balanced family-style meal with veg, protein + carbohydrates, possibly adapted
Before Bed	Before bed milk e.g. breast milk or cow's or fortified plant milks (if required)

Recipes

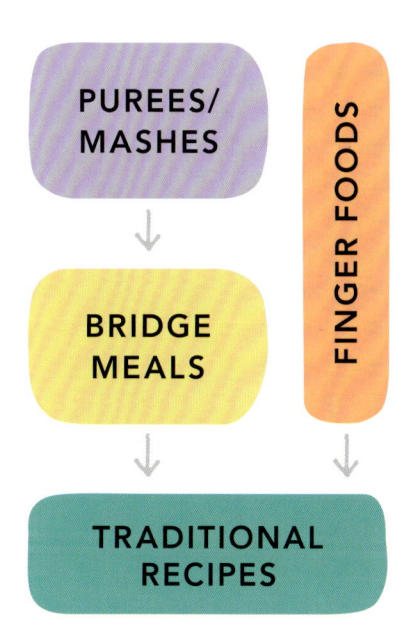

PUREES/MASHES

↓

BRIDGE MEALS

↓

FINGER FOODS

↓

TRADITIONAL RECIPES

These recipes aim to take you on a weaning journey. We start with purees and mashes to help ease you and your little one into the process of weaning, and then gently move on to more complex mashes in terms of their textures and amount of ingredients (see pages 45–53).

Next, we move on to what I call 'bridge meals' (pages 57–71), which help you move your baby from 'baby-style' foods to meals that are more centred on family mealtimes and the kinds of meals we might traditionally eat as a family. Bridge meals aren't essential if you've done baby-led weaning from the start (for example, you haven't offered mashes or purees) or your baby is super confident with weaning, but I think they help babies explore more and hone their eating skills, and, more importantly, start to accept more 'family-style' meals early on.

The next section offers plenty of finger food options – great for those of you who are baby-led weaning or want to offer your little one more finger foods early on. These also double up as nutritious snacks for toddlers over one and can help to add texture and variety into baby's meals and toddler's snack options. From here, we move on to the more traditional recipes, with breakfasts, lunches, dinners and celebratory food ideas – all designed to be made for adults and little ones alike, but with your baby and toddler in mind. These can be served to everyone in the family (though you might need to adapt some by adding a little extra flavour for the adults or mashing up some elements for younger babies here and there), and are all delicious, winning family favourites.

Because babies move through weaning and their food journey at such different paces, the recipes may need to be adapted more for some babies than others. So feel free to blend, mash, chop smaller or leave out ingredients if you're not sure your baby is ready for them – flexibility is key here. Versatility in ingredients is so important as it helps you to adapt recipes easily and make feeding your babies and toddlers super flexible. Please see the table on pages 40–1 for good swaps for allergens and other ingredients too. I really hope you love these recipes as much as I've enjoyed writing and testing them!

Charlotte xx

Symbols key*

Ve Vegan

  Includes nuts

d Includes dairy

  Includes wheat

g Includes gluten

O Includes egg

S Includes soy

  Includes fish

  Includes shellfish

Se Includes sesame

*I have marked the recipes with these symbols according to the main (first listed) ingredients, and assumed that a milk, spread or yoghurt 'of choice' can be non-dairy. If you or your little one has allergies, please read the recipes carefully.

What Equipment Do I Need?

At the very basic level you simply need:

- a chopping board
- a knife
- a fork/masher
- a grater
- a pan
- a soft spoon for baby

- equipment to blend (if starting with purees) e.g. a hand blender
- a bib
- a highchair
- cloths to clean up

In the recipes that follow, I quite often use a blender or food processor for mixing and grinding foods. You can use a hand-held stick blender or a baby food maker if it's easier for you and you have one. I do find a blender or food processor can make a lot of family meals easier to manage.

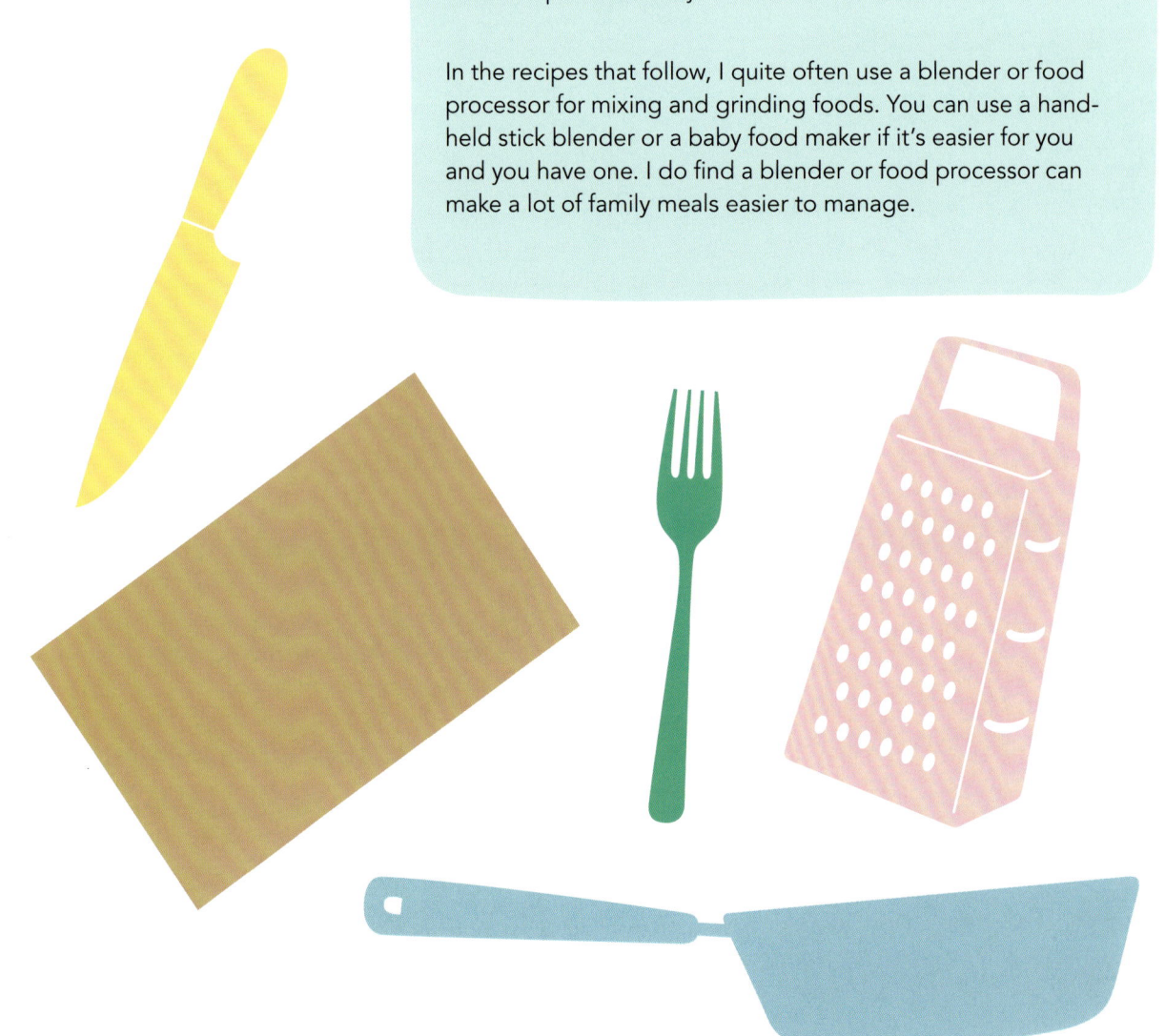

Food safety

- Always make sure you wash your hands. It's great to get little ones into the habit of this too, so try to wipe their hands with a soapy cloth or carry them to the sink for a quick clean up before meals.

- Keep kitchen surfaces and utensils clean.

- Practise food safety and hygiene practices before serving foods: for example, wash all fruit and vegetables.

- Avoid reheating foods more than once, especially rice.

- Always reheat food all the way through until piping hot and then let it cool before serving.

- Use different chopping boards for raw and cooked foods, especially meat and fish.

- Ensure leftover food is cooled and stored correctly as per recipe instructions.

- Pay attention to food date labelling. Use-by dates relate to food safety whereas best-before dates relate to food quality.

- If the dish includes an allergen, ensure you have already introduced it to your baby's diet safely (see page 24).

Alternative Ingredients/Substitutes

Ingredient	Alternative	Notes
Beans	• Different types of beans and chickpeas can be pretty much interchangeable. • You can also swap beans for tofu or small chunks of chicken or fish	Mixed beans can be a good way to add even more variety.
Butter	• Plant-based spreads • Olive oil	These alternatives usually work just as well as butter in cooking. Vary the types of fats you use.
Cheese	• Nutritional yeast • Dairy-free cheese • Tofu	Nutritional yeast won't replace the texture, but can add a cheesy flavour. Dairy-free cheese can work well, but it takes a bit of trial and error to find a good one. Use tofu in chunks.
Eggs	• Flaxseed or chia seed egg • 1 banana/apple sauce • Tofu • Egg replacement (from shop)	1 tbsp chia seeds or ground flaxseed with 3 tbsp warm water. Sit for 5 minutes until thickened. Use banana/apple sauce in sweet bakery products. Use tofu instead of scrambled egg.
Fish	• Swap for tofu, butter beans, chickpeas or chicken • Add avocado and/or olive oil for some omega-3 fatty acids	These alternatives won't work in all recipes, and often don't have the same flavour/texture, but can replace some of the nutrients.
Fresh herbs	• Dried herbs	Use roughly ⅓–¼ of the amount stated for fresh.
Garlic powder	• Garlic flakes • Garlic clove	The equivalent for ½ teaspoon of garlic powder is 1 fresh garlic clove.
Ground nuts	• Any ground nuts	You can stick with one or start to mix nuts and seeds once your baby has tried them all individually, like in my super seed recipe on page 125.
Ground seeds	• Any ground seeds	If using ground seeds to make 'egg replacer', chia seeds or flaxseed are the best options.
Meat	• Tofu • Lentils • Beans • Chickpeas • Quorn	Lots of these can replace the nutrients in meat, but not necessarily the texture/flavours. It's always good to vary the plant-based protein/iron sources you use in foods.

Ingredient	Alternative	Notes
Milk	• Usually any plant-based alternatives work well	Some are more watery, so may not thicken products as well. Aim for plain and fortified.
Milled seeds	No suitable alternatives	Quite often you can simply leave these out or add a little more dry matter (e.g. flour) to compensate.
Pasta	• Any other style of pasta • Rice or couscous • Gnocchi • Spiralised veg	These can all work well as replacements, but remember that spiralised veggies aren't a replacement for carbs, nutritionally, but can be a great, fresh alternative sometimes.
Peanut butters	• Any other nut butter • Tahini • NoNuts nut butter • Seed butters e.g., sunflower butter • Dairy butter or spread	You can find NoNuts nut butter online.
Plain flour	• Gluten-free flour • Ground almonds • Polenta	It's easy to swap these like for like in many recipes.
Quinoa	• Couscous • Buckwheat • Rice • Potatoes	Grains are super easy to swap; simply follow pack instructions to ensure they are cooked.
Root veggies	• Carrot/parsnips/butternut squash can be used interchangeably • Use frozen vegetable varieties as well	Some harder veg take longer to cook, so you might need to take this into account in the cooking time. Add frozen veggies in at the end of the recipe.
Self-raising flour	• Plain flour and baking powder	Add 2 teaspoons baking powder to 150g plain flour.
Soured cream	• Yoghurt • Crème fraîche	These usually work well as substitutes.
Tofu	• Meat • Chicken • Fish • Quorn • Beans • Eggs	If you're not a tofu fan, simply swap it for any of these. Meat and fish will need to be cooked according to packet instructions.

Purees and Mashes

In this section, you'll find some super simple ideas for your baby's first meals after their very first tastes of veggies (see page 13). The idea of these is to offer examples of next-step meals and different combinations of ingredients to help your baby in their journey with exploring a variety of foods. I've started with simple two-ingredient purees and then moved on to more complex combinations, upping the textures to help your little one progress. It's good to be mindful of moving gradually but stealthily through textures (see pages 16–17). If at any point you fancy trying a recipe but you want it mashed, not pureed, or vice versa, go for it. Follow your baby's lead with textures and adapt them as you see necessary, and remember, babies only really need purees for the first few weeks of weaning.

I usually try to add a protein-/iron-rich food to all of baby's main meals, so you'll see there are lots of beans, lentils and chickpeas. You can swap them for meat or other pulses, but they might need a little extra cooking time. You can add cow's milk (once introduced – see page 24), fortified plant milks or their usual breast or formula milk to any of these purees to help smooth, loosen or thin them out. Milk is helpful to add as it is familiar and provides extra nutrients. You could also add some milled seeds (in small amounts) or ground nuts, once your baby has had nuts (see page 23).

These recipes all offer examples of finger foods to have alongside the purees and mashes, so your baby has plenty of practice with self-feeding and exploring solid foods. If you want to do baby-led weaning, you could skip this section or offer purees with veggie sticks, toast fingers and pasta to scoop and self-feed. You'll see that I've included portion sizes in these recipes. I've based these on rough serving sizes, but, as always, please feed to appetite (see page 26).

Storing and reheating leftovers

These recipes will keep in the fridge for 1–2 days, in an airtight container, or in the freezer for around 2–3 months. Defrost thoroughly in the fridge overnight. If offering to baby warm, heat through until piping hot and then allow to cool before serving. Remember that your baby won't be on purees for very long, so you can always use up any frozen portions later as a dip or stirred into a sauce. If storing leftover rice, it must be cooled down within one hour, then placed into the fridge and consumed either hot or cold within 24 hours. If reheating rice, check it is steaming hot all the way through. Do not reheat rice more than once. If using pre-cooked microwave rice, do not store and reheat afterwards.

Carrot and Lentil Puree

Lentils are a great source of iron, which is a super important nutrient for young babies and toddlers, and so it's a good food to offer into their diet nice and early on in their weaning journey. This is a simple combo, though you could add a pinch of dried coriander or stir in some yoghurt if you wanted to try a different variation and add some extras. You can easily mash this instead of pureeing for a baby who needs more texture – just make sure the carrots are super soft, add a splash of liquid and then mash it well with the back of a fork.

Prep: 2 minutes
Cook: 12–16 minutes
Makes: about 2–3 portions for baby

2 medium carrots (about 175g), peeled and chopped into ½-cm thick batons
3 tbsp cooked puy lentils
2–3 tbsp water or milk of choice

1   Bring a small saucepan of water to the boil. Add the carrots and cook for 12–15 minutes (or until cooked through and soft enough to squidge flat when pressed between your finger and thumb). Add the lentils to the pan for the final minute to warm through.

2   Drain and carefully put a few carrot batons to one side to serve as finger food. Pop the rest of the carrots and lentils into a blender along with 2 tablespoons of the water (or milk).

3   Blend to form a smooth puree (adding a splash more water or milk to loosen if needed), scraping down the sides as necessary.

4   Serve with the reserved carrot batons and then store the remaining puree in an ice-cube tray for another day.

Adaptations for the whole family: This makes a nice dip for finger foods or veggie sticks. Or you could easily add this mix to a sauce or curry that you're making at a later date. Or have it as a soup with some nice crusty bread and add some seasoning.

Switching ingredients in/out: It's super easy to swap the lentils for beans or opt for a different veggie.

Tip: I prefer to use pre-cooked packs of lentils for ease, especially when cooking for my family. But if you prefer to use dried lentils, just soak or cook first according to the packet instructions.

Chicken, Green Beans and Pea Puree

If you want to offer meat to your baby, it's a good idea to introduce it early on so that they can become familiar with the flavour and texture. You can easily swap the chicken for extra drained butter beans if you want to keep it veggie or add plenty of extras too, such as cheese, ground nuts or extra veg. It also makes a good sauce you can serve with pasta fingers for any of you doing baby-led weaning. This is a really easy one to adapt the texture too – just add a little more liquid if you want it to be a thinner puree or less if you'd like it a little thicker. Don't be afraid to experiment with the textures your baby will accept.

Prep: 2 minutes
Cook: 10–15 minutes
Makes: about 4 portions for baby

1 free-range skinless and boneless chicken breast (about 180g), cut into strips
50g green beans, trimmed and halved (fresh or frozen)
2 tbsp frozen peas
3 tbsp water or milk of choice
3 tbsp tinned butter beans, drained and rinsed (optional)

1 Bring a small saucepan of water to the boil. Add the chicken and cook for 10–15 minutes (or until cooked through), adding the green beans and peas for the final 5 minutes.

2 Drain, and carefully put a few green beans and chicken strips to one side to serve as finger food. Pop the rest of the ingredients into a blender along with 2 tablespoons of the water (or milk).

3 Add the butter beans (if using) and blend to form a smooth puree (adding a splash more water or milk to loosen if needed), scraping down the sides as necessary.

4 Serve with the reserved green beans and chicken strips and then store the remaining puree in an ice-cube tray for another day.

Adaptations for the whole family: This works well as a pasta sauce (just add some seasoning for the adults) or leave a few more finger foods and eat the chicken sticks and green beans along with your baby so they can watch and learn how to eat from you!

Beef, Rice and Courgette Puree

This is a good one to add in some meat for your baby to help them get used to the taste and texture, while also adding all-important nutrients such as iron and zinc. If you're after a veggie option, swap the beef for kidney beans and just mash them up before cooking. I *love* using mashes to make balls for babies too – this one works really well with the rice blended less and rolled into little balls for your little one to try to navigate. It's a great way for them to explore food and self-feeding.

Prep: 10 minutes
Cook: 10–12 minutes
Makes: about 2–3 portions for baby

150g beef mince
½ courgette (about 75g), very finely grated
40g pre-cooked rice
small pinch of paprika (optional)
1 tbsp olive oil

1 In a bowl, add the mince, courgette and rice. Give it a good mix and mash together. Add the paprika if you fancy adding more flavour.

2 If you want to offer your baby finger food, roll some of the mixture into balls. Heat the oil in a frying pan and add the mince mixture (including any that you've made into balls). Cook for around 10 minutes until the mixture is brown, the balls are nice and golden and cooked through and the juices run clear.

3 Once cooked, put the balls to one side and add the rest of the mixture to a small blender. Whizz to form a paste/mash.

4 Serve the puree with a few balls on the side.

Adaptations for the whole family: Add extra paprika and have as balls with a little side salad and a chunky tomato salsa.

Tip: If offering this mix again, why not add a tiny bit of peanut butter to test for allergies or mash in a small amount of cooked egg (see the allergy guidelines on page 24).

Beef, Rice and Courgette Puree

Chicken, Green Beans and Pea Puree

Red Pepper with Spinach and Bean Puree

Pear, Banana and Oat Puree

'My Kinda' Dhal Mash

Carrot and Lentil Puree

Salmon, Greens and Potato Mash

Broccoli, Potato and Cheese Mash

'My Kinda' Dhal Mash

Ve

It's *so* good to help babies explore different flavours in their foods, even early on, and this is my little take on a dhal for a young baby. Start nice and small – go in with a pinch of curry powder to start with and build on those flavours as your baby gets more familiar with them. This recipe is a little thicker, trying to help your little one to explore textures a little more, so I recommend just mashing this. If you find it's a bit too thick for your baby, add some liquid, such as milk or water, and mash again, or blend it. (Note: It can be tricky to find no added salt curry powder. As it's such a small amount, it's OK if you only have curry powder with salt in it – just be mindful of how much you use in your baby's portion.)

Prep: 5 minutes
Cook: 10–12 minutes
Makes: about 2 portions for baby

1 sweet potato (about 200g), peeled
3 tbsp (about 60g) tinned chickpeas, drained, rinsed and mashed
pinch–¼ tsp no added salt mild curry powder

> **Tip:** If freezing, ideally freeze before adding the curry powder as this can somewhat intensify over time.

1 Bring a medium saucepan of water to the boil.

2 Slice a quarter of the sweet potato into thick wedges and the rest into 1-cm chunks.

3 Add the sweet potato to the pan and cook for 8–10 minutes (or until cooked through and soft enough to squidge flat when pressed between your finger and thumb).

4 Add the chickpeas to the pan to warm through for 1–2 minutes. Drain, and carefully put the sweet potato wedges to one side to serve as finger food.

5 Pour the rest of the sweet potato back into the pan with the chickpeas and mash to make a chunky puree. Add some liquid such as milk or water if you want to make it looser. Stir in the curry powder and serve in a bowl with some of the sweet potato wedges on the side.

Adaptations for the whole family: It's easy to double/triple up the ingredients here and make it into a dhal for the whole family. Add some extra flavours, extra veggies and some tinned tomatoes. Or it's delicious as it is, swept up with a pitta bread or served in a wrap with some spinach, cucumber and a little mango chutney. Add a little extra curry powder to the mash, if needed.

Switching ingredients in/out: Swap the chickpeas for lentils or butter beans if you have them to use up. Use potatoes, squash or any other veggies instead of the sweet potato if you prefer.

Broccoli, Potato and Cheese Mash

~~~~~~~~~~~~~~~~~~~~~~~~~~~~~~~~~~~~~

This super simple recipe often goes a long way with little ones. Ada has always loved mashed potato and I like to add extras to it to bulk out the nutrients she has with her meals. This one includes an allergen – dairy – so start with a tiny amount of cheese if your little one has never had any dairy before and follow the allergy guidelines on page 24.

 Prep: 5 minutes | **Cook:** 12–15 minutes
Makes: about 2–3 portions for baby

100g broccoli, cut into small florets
1 medium baking potato (about 200g),
  peeled and cut into 2-cm chunks
15g Cheddar cheese, grated

1   Bring a small saucepan of water to the boil. Add the broccoli and potato and cook for 12–15 minutes (or until cooked through and soft enough to squidge flat when pressed between your finger and thumb).

2   Drain, and carefully put a few florets of broccoli to one side to serve as finger food.

3   Leave the rest of the broccoli and potato to steam-dry and then pop them back into the pan, mash really well and add in the cheese, mixing it all together. You can add a splash of milk or some of the cooking water if the mash needs loosening a little.

4   Serve the mash with a few of the reserved broccoli florets on the side.

Adaptations for the whole family: This works well as a mash in your own meal – add extra cheese and seasoning if you prefer. It also makes potato tots for older kids too. Simply roll the mixture into tots and bake in the oven (preheat to 200°C/180°C fan) for 15 minutes, or until they are a little more solid on the outside, and serve!

Pear, Banana and Oat Puree

~~~~~~~~~~~~~~~~~~~~~~~~~~~~~~~~~~~~~

This is a take on breakfast which is super tasty and easy to adapt for yourself too. You can add some allergens into it such as ground nuts or nut butters, in small amounts (see the allergy guidelines on page 24). This is a great one for exploring textures – you can use the oats whole and mash the fruits less, adding less milk to make the texture a bit thicker and lumpier. You could add a dollop of yoghurt when serving too.

 Prep: 5 minutes | **Cook:** 2–3 minutes
Makes: about 1–2 portions for baby

4 tbsp porridge oats
1 ripe pear, peeled (plus ½ ripe pear for finger food)
½ ripe banana, peeled (plus ½ ripe banana for
  finger food)
splash of milk of choice

1   Put the oats in a blender and whizz until they have a rough, flour-like texture.

2   In a bowl, mash the pear and banana together really well.

3   Add the oats and milk and mix together. (Add another splash of milk if it feels a little dry.)

4   Serve cold or warm through in a pan for a few minutes, stirring in another splash of milk to loosen, if needed.

5   Serve with some finger-shaped sticks of banana and some peeled soft pear fingers.

Adaptations for the whole family: Double up this recipe and have some for yourself too! Don't blend the oats and simply cook for a few minutes in a pan, and serve with a dollop of yoghurt and a drizzle of honey. Alternatively, add the ingredients to a smoothie with some extra milk and yoghurt.

Tip: Oats don't fair too well when frozen, so I wouldn't freeze this!

Salmon, Greens and Potato Mash

This one is a bit of a freestyle recipe – you can add in whatever leftover greens you have and add a pinch of extra flavours or cheese if you want. If using kale or tougher greens, make sure you de-stalk and rip the leaves into little pieces first before cooking.

Prep: 5 minutes
Cook: 10–12 minutes, or 20 minutes if serving as fishcakes
Makes: about 2–3 portions for baby

1 medium potato, peeled and chopped into 2-cm pieces
30g greens, such as peas, spinach or kale (or other leafy green veg), washed, stems removed (if necessary) and finely chopped
100g sustainable skinless and boneless salmon fillet, cut into 2-cm chunks
1 tbsp olive oil, if serving as fishcakes and frying

1 Bring a medium saucepan pan of water to the boil. Add the potato, greens and salmon.

2 Cook for around 10–12 minutes, or until the fish and potato are cooked through, then drain everything and mash it all together really well. If you've used some tough leaves, try blending these a little first with a splash of water to make it more manageable for your baby and then mash it in with the potato and salmon.

3 Offer as a simple mash or as mini fishcakes: shape the mixture into burgers, preheat the oil in a frying pan and cook the fishcakes for 5 minutes on each side until golden.

Adaptations for the whole family: Add a good grating of cheese to the mix and enjoy as fishcakes, served with a salad. Alternatively, serve as potato mash on the side of your usual lunch or dinner. Older kids will also enjoy this served as fishcakes.

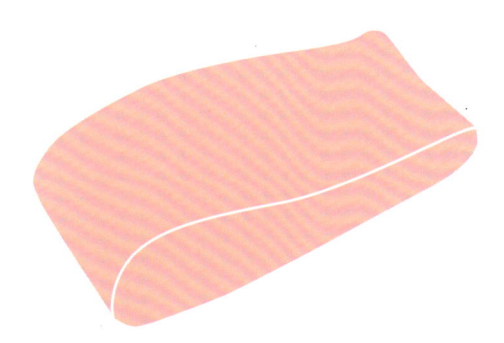

Red Pepper with Spinach and Bean Puree

Red pepper is one of my favourite foods for babies, so I do try to include it in a good few recipes or as a finger food on the side (cooked and sliced). This recipe adds a real mix of flavours for your baby's taste buds to explore. It's a really fab one and can easily be added to and bulked out and turned into a chilli-style meal. This one isn't so easy to mash, but you can blend it or even mash the beans and add them to the blended pepper and spinach instead. You can serve it with other finger food sticks or even spread it on a little toast as a finger food for baby.

Prep: 2 minutes
Cook: 8–10 minutes
Makes: about 2–3 portions for baby

splash of olive oil
50g red pepper, deseeded and cut into rough small pieces
handful of spinach (about 25g), washed
pinch–¼ tsp ground cumin
50g white beans, such as butter or cannellini beans, drained and rinsed
1–2 tbsp water or milk of choice
1 slice of good-quality bread (wholemeal if possible), toasted and cut into strips

1 Heat the oil in a small frying pan over a medium heat. Add the pepper, spinach and cumin. Cook for 8–10 minutes, stirring occasionally.

2 Once cooked, pour the mixture into a small blender and add the beans and a splash of water or milk. Blend to a thick consistency.

3 Serve the puree with a few toast fingers or spread on toast soldiers.

Adaptations for the whole family: This is perfect as a dip for adults. Add some extras if needed or serve in a heated wrap with crunchy slaw and hot sauce. Alternatively, it can be served over a jacket potato. This puree can be stirred through pasta for older children.

Bridge Meals

This section introduces a brand-new concept from me – bridge meals! I know that, sometimes, it can feel a little daunting to go straight from giving your baby mashes to serving up meals that you eat as a family in their entirety, so these bridge meals will help you start to gradually and gently introduce more of the ingredients, textures and flavours of 'family-style' meals to your little one. Of course, if you feel confident and your baby has taken really well to solids and is exploring lots of finger foods, you may feel like you don't need bridge meals and be confident to go straight to the next sections of this book, which is completely fine.

These recipes are designed to be adaptable, simple transition foods for babies, often using more basic or a smaller number of ingredients, or quicker methods with smaller portion sizes. All of this is easy to change, though, and they can be doubled up and served to the whole family.

I hope you like these bridge meals. If you're looking for finger food options to offer alongside these, I've suggested how to offer some of these recipes as finger foods or you can always serve some of the finger foods I've created on pages 75–107 too!

Storing and reheating leftovers

These recipes will keep in the fridge for 2 days, in an airtight container, or in the freezer for 3 months. To defrost, remove from the freezer and allow to thoroughly defrost in the fridge overnight. If offering to baby warm, heat through until piping hot and then allow to cool before serving. Remember that your baby won't be on purees for very long, so you can always use up any frozen portions later as a dip or stirred into a sauce. If eating leftover rice, it must have been cooled down quickly (within one hour) and then placed in the fridge and consumed either hot or cold within 24 hours. If reheating rice, check it is steaming hot all the way through. Do not reheat rice more than once.

Mini Chicken Pie

This works so well as a really simplified version of a pie and is super easy to adapt too. You can add a little more flavour or veggies as your baby gets more familiar with this dish or as they get older (or for your own portions). It's easy, delicious and filling, and is good for making in bulk too!

Prep: 5 minutes
Cook: 20–25 minutes
Serves: 1 adult and
2 babies/toddlers

1 free-range skinless and boneless chicken breast (about 200g), sliced into strips
2 medium potatoes (about 400g), peeled and chopped into even chunks
2 spring onions, trimmed and finely chopped
small handful of frozen peas and/or spinach (about 50g), finely chopped
2 tbsp milk of choice
40g mature Cheddar cheese, grated (optional)

Serving ideas: Serve with some green veggies on the side.

Tip: Ideally freeze in portions pre-grilling.

1 Bring two large saucepans of water to the boil. Add the chicken to one and poach for 10–15 minutes, until it's cooked all the way through. Then drain and remove the chicken to the side. Add the potatoes to the other pan and cook for 12–15 minutes, until they are soft enough to stab with a knife.

2 Add the spring onions, peas and/or spinach to the pan with the potatoes for the final 3 minutes to cook.

3 Preheat the grill. Add the chicken to a 20cm round ovenproof dish or divide it between little ramekins.

4 Drain the potatoes, spring onions and peas and/or spinach. Leave to steam-dry for a few minutes and then pour them back into the pan. Add the milk and mash well.

5 Top the cooked chicken with the potato mash and the cheese (if using).

6 Pop under the grill for 5 minutes (or until the top is beginning to get nice and golden).

7 Leave to cool before serving. You might want to serve your baby's portion with the parts separated out so they can grab the chicken pieces as finger food. Alternatively, offer it with a spoon and break down the chicken in the base first, if your baby needs it.

Adaptations for the whole family: Add seasoning to the mash when dividing it out into ramekins or add extra cheese to the adult portions if you're used to a little more salt in your foods.

Switching ingredients in/out: You can easily swap the chicken for salmon. Just use a 200g fillet, cut into strips, and fry in a little oil for around 8–10 minutes, until cooked through.

Images overleaf →

Charlotte's Lasagnette

This is such an exciting recipe for me. It's a simplified version of a lasagne, which is delicious and super nutritious and all made in a single pan! I actually created one of these recipes with Little Dish, and wanted to include a more simplified version in this book so you can all try it at home. This works so well for the whole family too, so it's a good one to batch-cook and make in bulk. You can easily vary the veg or the proteins you use to make it how you like it.

Prep: 10 minutes
Cook: 20–25 minutes
Serves: 1 adult and
2 babies/toddlers

drizzle of olive oil
1 garlic clove, peeled and
  finely grated
1 small onion (about 60g),
  peeled and finely chopped
150g beef mince or 100g
  diced mushrooms
1 carrot, grated (optional)
400g tin chopped tomatoes
50g pre-cooked puy lentils (or
  100g if using mushrooms
  instead of beef)
110g fresh lasagne sheets,
  cut into 2.5-cm squares
40g cheese, grated (Cheddar
  or mozzarella work well)

1. Preheat the oven to 180°C/160°C fan, then heat the oil in a 23cm ovenproof frying pan over a medium heat.

2. Add the garlic and onion and cook for a few minutes, giving them a stir, before adding the beef mince. If using mushrooms and/or carrot, add them now.

3. Cook, stirring occasionally to combine it all, for around 6–8 minutes.

4. Add the tomatoes and puy lentils. Swirl 150 millilitres of water in the empty tomato tin and then pour it into the pan. Stir to combine, turn up the heat and let it bubble away for 1 minute, then turn down and simmer for another 4–5 minutes.

5. Once the sauce has thickened a little, slowly add in the cut-up lasagne sheets, sprinkling them into the sauce as you stir so they don't stick together.

6. Even out the top of the sauce, sprinkle with the cheese and pop in the oven for 10 minutes until golden and bubbling.

7. Leave a portion to cool for your baby/toddler and serve as it is, letting them dissect it and feed themselves, or give it a little mash or chop, if needed, and offer to them with a spoon.

Adaptations for the whole family: This is perfect as it is, though you might want to season or add more cheese to your portion, or double the recipe for the whole family.

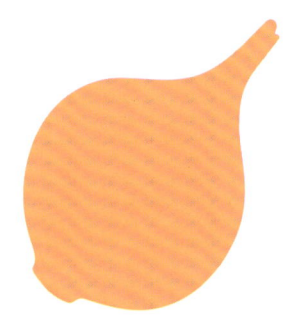

Tomato Orzo

I love orzo and it's actually a really great 'bridge' ingredient for babies as it can be super soft and easier to eat than whole pieces of pasta. This is such an easy win and can be adapted, bulked out or turned into a bigger meal for the whole family. This is a good way of offering some tofu too, which is a really nutritious food for babies and a great ingredient to introduce during weaning.

Prep: 5 minutes
Cook: 15–16 minutes
Serves: 1 adult and
1–2 babies/toddlers

½ tbsp olive oil
½ coloured pepper, deseeded and finely chopped
¼ tsp dried oregano
75g orzo
200ml passata/tinned chopped tomatoes or 200g fresh tomatoes, finely chopped
75g firm tofu, roughly crumbled

1   Heat the oil in a small saucepan over a medium heat. Add the chopped pepper and oregano and fry for 4–5 minutes, stirring now and then. Add the orzo and tomatoes and give the mixture a stir before adding 100 millilitres of water.

2   Leave it to bubble away with the lid on for 10 minutes, checking halfway that it is not catching on the bottom of the pan. Give it a stir and add a splash more water if necessary.

3   Once the orzo is cooked and the mixture has thickened, stir in the tofu. Once cooled a little, serve in a bowl to your baby with a spoon.

Adaptations for the whole family: Season the mixture a little, stir through some spinach until it wilts and add a drizzle of olive oil or balsamic vinegar on top. You might also like to sprinkle over a little grated Parmesan or Cheddar cheese.

Tip: To make things easier, you can use frozen peppers.

Plum and Banana Crumble Bake

This is a super easy and quick version of a crumble as a 'bridge meal' for your baby. Of course, they can have a regular crumble you make at home too (without the sugar!), but this works as a lovely segue into crumbles and is perfect for brekkie, pudding or even as a snack! My family really liked this one. It's also easy to change up the fruits – so swap plums for peaches or pears or any other stone fruit. You will need to use ripe plums in this. If you can't get hold of these, they might just need to cook for a little longer.

Prep: 6 minutes
Cook: 8–10 minutes
Serves: 1 adult and 2 babies/toddlers

4 ripe plums, destoned and finely diced
juice of 1 large orange (about 3–4 tbsp) or 3–4 tbsp orange juice from a carton
2 tbsp porridge oats
1 small banana, peeled and mashed
2 tbsp ground nuts (for example, almonds, pistachios or cashews) or my Super Duper Seed Mix (see page 125)
natural yoghurt or dairy-free alternative, to serve

1 Add the plums to a small saucepan with the orange juice, oats and 2 tablespoons of water. Cover with a lid and cook over a medium heat for 8 minutes, stirring occasionally. This will soften the plums and cook the oats (it might take more or less time, and you might need to add a little more water, depending on how ripe the plums are).

2 Once the plums are cooked and softened, stir in the banana.

3 You can either serve the crumble in a bowl with the ground nuts sprinkled on top and a dollop of yoghurt, or you can decant it into an ovenproof dish, pop it under the grill for 1–2 minutes to toast the nutty topping and then serve with a dollop of yoghurt.

Serving ideas: Serve with some extra banana fingers on the side.

Adaptations for the whole family: Serve with a little honey and more yoghurt.

Tip: If offering these specific nuts for the first time, ensure you follow the allergy guidance on page 24.

Salmon and Dill Couscous

This is a simple way of offering some oily fish to your baby and is a delicious meal for other family members too. Couscous can be quite a challenging texture for babies as they have to work out how to deal with little bits of food in their mouth. Mixing the yoghurt through might help them to manage it a little better. This is such a tasty combination for babies, toddlers and adults.

Prep: 5 minutes
Cook: 12 minutes
Serves: 1 adult and
2 babies/toddlers

80g wholewheat couscous
    or quinoa
1 lemon
½ tbsp olive oil
2 x 130g sustainable skinless
    and boneless salmon or
    white fish fillets
a couple of sprigs of dill,
    finely chopped
3–4 tbsp yoghurt or dairy-free
    alternative

1 Cook the couscous according to the packet instructions. Once cooked, zest and juice half the lemon and stir it through the cooked couscous.

2 Heat the oil in a medium frying pan, add the fish and cook for 8–10 minutes (or until cooked through), flipping halfway through cooking so it cooks on both sides.

3 Mix the dill into the yoghurt and add a little extra squeeze of lemon.

4 Either flake the cooked salmon into the couscous or serve the couscous with salmon pieces on the side. Add a tablespoon of the dill yoghurt on the side too.

Adaptations for the whole family: Serve the couscous with extra herbs stirred through it, add seasoning and a handful of avocado chunks or dressed salad leaves.

Spiced Scrambled Eggs

This really simple twist on scrambled eggs adds extra colour and flavours to your baby's brekkie or toast topping, helping them to experience more variety. Scrambled eggs is such a quick option and it's also a good texture to experiment with during weaning. As with the 'My Kinda' Dhal Mash on page 50, it can be tricky to find no added salt curry powder. It's OK if you only have curry powder with salt in it – just be mindful of how much you use in your baby's portion.

Prep: 5 minutes
Cook: 5 minutes
Serves: 1 adult and
2 babies/toddlers

3 large free-range eggs,
  or 100g firm tofu, crumbled
½ tsp ground turmeric
½ tsp no added salt mild curry
  powder
1 tsp olive oil
pinch of black onion seeds
  (optional)

1 Crack the eggs or place the tofu into a bowl, add the spices and whisk until combined.

2 Heat the oil in a small frying pan over a low-medium heat, add the whisked eggs or tofu and cook for 5 minutes, stirring occasionally.

3 Sprinkle with the onion seeds (if using) and serve.

Serving ideas: Serve with toast fingers and some ripe avocado or soft cooked red pepper slices.

Adaptations for the whole family: Serve in a heated wrap with crunchy slaw and hot sauce, or with toast and a little chilli sauce.

Tip: If offering eggs for the first time, remember to follow the allergy guidelines on page 24.

Creamy Lentil Pasta

This is a fab one-pan meal! It's also great for helping your baby to explore new textures and some new, cheesy flavours. Pasta can be such an easy staple for toddlers, so offering it early and getting them familiar with it is a good idea. You may need to give this a good mash with the back of a fork for young babies who are still very much exploring textures. Keep a couple of pieces of pasta unmashed so your baby can have a go at self-feeding too. As your baby gets more familiar with pasta, you can stop mashing and try other shapes.

Prep: 5 minutes
Cook: 10–12 minutes (pasta depending)
Serves: 2 adults and 2 babies/toddlers

200g pasta, such as fusilli
1 courgette, coarsely grated
150g pre-cooked lentils
3 tbsp full-fat cream cheese or dairy-free alternative
1–2 large pinches of dried thyme
65g mature Cheddar cheese, coarsely grated (optional)
zest of ½ lemon (optional)

1 Cook the pasta according to the packet instructions.

2 When the pasta has 5 minutes left, pop the courgette into the pan to cook through.

3 Drain the pasta and courgette, reserving some of the starchy pasta water and a couple of pieces of pasta to serve as finger food, and pop the rest of the pasta and the courgette back into the pan. Add the lentils, cream cheese, thyme and cheese (if using) and stir well (give it a mash for younger babies).

4 Serve sprinkled with the lemon zest (if using), alongside the reserved pasta pieces as finger foods.

Adaptations for the whole family: Add a little extra cheese on top or some capers and a handful of rocket stirred through before serving. For older kids, swap the courgette for other veg or grate in extra veggies.

Tip: Freeze this one *before* mashing so you can give it to your baby when they are a little older and used to textures.

Creamy Mushroom Toast Topping

If you've followed me for a while, you'll probably see that I'm a big fan of mushrooms! Ada loves them too. Sometimes, though, they can be a bit of a tricky texture for little ones, so I like to introduce them early in the weaning journey so they can get used to the different flavour and texture. This is a really easy and delicious take on a mushroom stroganoff, and it can be offered in multiple ways – on toast or as a proper stroganoff with rice or potatoes.

Prep: 5 minutes
Cook: 15 minutes
Serves: 1 adult and 1 baby/toddler

1 tbsp olive oil
handful of chestnut mushrooms (about 160g), very finely chopped (or chopped and blended for smaller babies)
1 spring onion, trimmed and finely chopped
1 heaped tbsp plain flour
180ml milk of choice (plus 50ml more if you're serving it as a sauce)
a few squeezes of lemon
2–3 sprigs of flat-leaf parsley, finely chopped

1 Heat the oil in a medium frying pan over a medium heat.

2 Add the mushrooms and spring onions and cook for 8–10 minutes, stirring regularly until they are cooked and getting golden.

3 Add the flour and mix to combine, before stirring in the milk to form a thick, spreadable mix to go on toast. Alternatively, add the extra milk to serve it as a sauce.

4 Finish with a squeeze of lemon and the flat-leaf parsley, and stir again before serving.

Serving ideas: Serve with toast fingers, rice or potato fingers.

Adaptations for the whole family: This is delicious as it is, but you could add some Parmesan, a little extra lemon juice and a grind of black pepper to give it more 'zing'.

Super Simple Chilli

 Ve

A chilli is such a fab, balanced meal for little ones and, as a family, we love it. This recipe is a *super* simple adaptation of a 'chilli' that you can easily bulk out and add to as your baby gets more efficient at eating. When your little one is just starting out on their weaning journey, they won't be able to cope with a lot of hot spices, so it's good to go easy at first, but, in time, you can be a bit more experimental with the paprika.

Prep: 5 minutes
Cook: 5 minutes
Serves: 1 adult and 2 babies/toddlers

120g tinned kidney beans (or other beans), drained and rinsed
pinch of smoked paprika
130g tinned chopped tomatoes or passata or fresh tomatoes, finely chopped
6 tbsp cooked wholegrain rice (optional)

1 Mash the kidney beans really well in a bowl with the paprika (or blend if needed).

2 Add the tomatoes and mix, mashing more to combine.

3 Add in the rice if using – or you can serve this alongside.

4 Heat the mixture in a pan (or microwave) until piping hot. Give it another mash if needed, but keep some texture in.

5 Allow to cool, then serve. If serving the rice alongside, you can mash a little, if needed.

Adaptations for the whole family: Spread onto toast and sprinkle with a little feta, rocket and lemon juice or simply don't mash your portion and have it as it is. For older kids, mash the mixture less and add in some extra veggies such as sweetcorn or chopped mushrooms.

Tip: If you're looking for a baby-led weaning option, try spreading a little of the chilli on some toast fingers.

Quinoa and Sweetcorn Salad

I'm all about offering new and exciting ingredients to expand a baby's palate and this one works really well. It's light and fresh, and is a lovely one for parents too. Fennel is a unique taste, so if you think your little one might be unsure, go in with a smaller amount and add extra to your own portion!

Prep: 10 minutes
Cook: 20–25 minutes
Serves: 1 adult and
1–2 babies/toddlers

60g quinoa
40g tinned chickpeas,
    drained and rinsed
2 tbsp tinned sweetcorn,
    drained
½ ripe avocado, mashed
35g fennel, finely grated
a few basil leaves, finely
    chopped

1   Cook the quinoa according to the packet instructions.

2   Once cooked, drain and leave to cool a little. Meanwhile, add the chickpeas and sweetcorn to a blender and pulse to break them down nicely (or just give them a good mash together with a fork or a pestle and mortar), then add them to a bowl with the avocado and fennel.

3   Finally, stir in the basil and the cooked quinoa, and give it all a good mix.

4   You can serve this to your baby on a spoon, which works well as the avocado pulls it all together, or try rolling it into tablespoon-sized balls and letting them feed themselves.

Serving ideas: If you want to serve extra finger food alongside, you could offer your baby some avocado slices on the side.

Adaptations for the whole family: This salad is really tasty as it is, but if you want something a bit different, try stuffing the mixture into a deseeded, pre-cooked pepper half and topping it with a little halloumi. Grill until golden. Alternatively, simply drizzle over a little of your favourite dressing and serve with some feta cheese. For older kids, keep things more chunky and don't puree it all.

Tip: Add a little lemon juice to stop the avocado browning so quickly. Mashed avocado isn't really suitable for freezing.

Finger Food and Snacks

Finger foods are such an important part of weaning. Helping your little one learn to self-feed via a variety of different finger foods can be so brilliant for their skill development and for helping them learn to be efficient little eaters fairly quickly during their weaning journey.
In this section, I've included a variety of simple finger foods. Some work well as mini meals on their own for babies, while others are good as meal accompaniments for older kids.

A lot of the textures I've included here are experimental, but that's what weaning is all about, and you'll soon find that, with plenty of practice and experience, your baby can start to easily eat a really wide variety of finger food options.

The best thing about most of these recipes is that, once your baby is nice and familiar with them, they also double up as helpful snacks (many of them on-the-go snacks) and, as a mum of two, I certainly know how helpful out and about, nutrient-rich and tasty snacks can be for fuelling and filling up little ones. It's always been something I've struggled with as I don't think a lot of shop-bought snacks cut it from a nutritional and filling-up standpoint.

I really hope you find these recipes helpful for weaning and way beyond!

Sweet Potato Twists

I absolutely love these twists. They are an alternative to bread or pastry, and you can make them into whatever you prefer: pinwheels, pizzas or tear-and-share platters. Here I've kept them simple as little twists, but have added extras with the courgette and toppings.

Prep: 5 minutes
Cook: 25–30 minutes
Makes: 12–14 twists

450g sweet potatoes, peeled and chopped into 2-cm cubes
½ tbsp olive oil
50g courgette, coarsely grated
125g self-raising flour, plus extra for dusting
handful of ground nuts/seeds (optional)

1 Preheat the oven to 200°C/180°C fan and pop the sweet potato cubes onto a tray. Drizzle with the oil and bake for 15–20 minutes, or until cooked through.

2 Mash the sweet potato or mix it in a blender to create a thick paste.

3 Squeeze the grated courgette in between your hands so that you get as much liquid out as possible, then add to a bowl along with the sweet potato. Give it a good mix, then add in the flour. Shape the mixture into a ball of dough.

4 Transfer the dough to a floured surface. Using a rolling pin, roll out the dough to form a sheet, roughly 20 x 30cm (about ½cm thick) and cut it into 10–12 long (3cm wide) strips.

5 Line another baking tray and pop each strip onto the tray, twisting it gently as you lay it down so you create a cheese straw kind of shape. Sprinkle with the ground nuts or seeds (if using).

6 Bake in the middle of the oven for 10 minutes, or until golden and smelling delicious.

7 Remove from the oven and allow to cool before serving.

Adaptations for the whole family: Spread some passata and cheese on the rolled out dough before cutting. You can try so many different toppings – I like sesame seeds or dried chilli flakes.

Storing leftovers: Cool to room temperature within 2 hours. Place into an airtight container in the fridge and eat within 2 days.

Image overleaf →

Fruit and Veg Flapjack

Flapjacks are such a great food for babies and toddlers as on-the-go snacks, finger foods or a packed lunch option, and they are bursting with energy and nutrients too – such a winner! I've created a few flapjack recipes in my time, including savoury ones, but I love this extra fruity one, which has such a mix of flavours, from the nut butter to the beetroot and ginger.

Prep: 10 minutes
Cook: 30 minutes
Makes: 16 flapjack squares or fingers

2 tbsp chia seeds
4 tbsp warm water
120g unsalted butter or plant-based spread
50g runny, smooth peanut butter
1 medium apple (about 120g), cored and grated
100g vacuum-packed beetroot in natural juices, drained and coarsely grated
250g porridge oats
1½ tsp ground ginger
handful of fresh raspberries or blueberries (about 50g), roughly mashed, plus extra to serve

1   In a small bowl, mix the chia seeds with the warm water and leave to one side.

2   Preheat the oven to 210°C/190°C fan and line a 20 x 20cm ovenproof tin with greaseproof paper.

3   Melt the butter in a medium saucepan, then add the peanut butter and heat to melt together, combining with a spoon. Take off the heat and add in the grated apple and beetroot.

4   Add the chia seed mix, oats, ginger and raspberries, and give it a good mix.

5   Decant into the lined tin, pressing down firmly with the back of a spoon to level off the top. Bake in the middle of the oven for 30 minutes, or until golden. Remove and leave to cool in the tin for at least 30 minutes before cutting into 16 flapjack squares.

6   Serve with a few extra raspberries mashed on top for a jammy texture and some extra sweetness if you wish.

Adaptations for the whole family: These are delicious with a dollop of yoghurt on the side.

Switching ingredients in/out: Swap the raspberries for blueberries. You can use 1–2 eggs instead of the chia seed and water. You can swap the ginger for cinnamon or nutmeg if you prefer.

Storing leftovers/how to defrost: Cool to room temperature within 2 hours. Place into an airtight container in the fridge and eat within 2 days. Alternatively, place in the freezer and consume within 3 months. Defrost in the fridge overnight or until fully thawed.

Pork Potato Tots with Red Pepper Dip

Potato tots are a classic baby and toddler recipe – they are so versatile as you can add all sorts into them, like fish or multiple chopped or grated veggies. These are made with pork or lentils, but you could easily use any other meat or pulses. Potato tots are a fab early finger food as they squash nicely but also hold their shape well. I love offering a dip with finger foods and this red pepper one is a winner you can use over and over again!

Prep: 10 minutes
Cook: 1 hour and 25 minutes
Makes: 12 tots and about 225g red pepper dip

1 large jacket potato (about 230g)
drizzle of olive oil
150g pork mince or pre-cooked/tinned lentils, drained and rinsed
30g tinned butter beans, drained, rinsed and mashed
¼ tsp garlic powder or 1 garlic clove, peeled and crushed

For the red pepper dip:
1 red pepper
110g tinned butter beans, drained and rinsed

1   Preheat the oven to 220°C/200°C fan. Wrap the potato in foil, place on a baking tray and bake for 1 hour until cooked and softened. After 30 minutes, pierce the pepper with a fork a few times and add it to the baking tray with the potato. Once cooked, remove and leave both to one side.

2   Meanwhile, heat the oil in a frying pan over a medium heat, then add the pork mince and cook for 3–4 minutes, stirring occasionally until cooked (skip this step if using lentils).

3   Once the potato is cooled a little, scrape out the inside and mash with the cooked mince (or lentils), mashed butter beans and garlic powder.

4   Line another baking tray with greaseproof paper.

5   Wet your hands slightly and form the potato mix into little tot shapes and bake on the lined tray for 12–14 minutes, or until golden. Turn them halfway through baking.

6   Meanwhile, make the pepper dip. Remove the seeds and stalk from the pepper once it's cool enough to touch, and pop in a blender with the butter beans. Whizz to form a thick dip. Add a few splashes of water if it's very thick.

7   Remove the tots from the oven and allow them to cool before serving with the pepper dip.

Adaptations for the whole family: These are fab as they are as a little snack for you too, though you might like to add some sweet chilli sauce to the dip.

Storing leftovers/how to defrost: Cool to room temperature within 2 hours. Place into an airtight container in the fridge and eat within 2 days. Alternatively, place in the freezer and consume within 3 months. Defrost in the fridge overnight or until fully thawed. Reheat until piping hot and then allow to cool before serving.

Tip: Once the ingredients are mashed together, you might want to skip making them into tots and offer your baby the mash on a spoon or simply roll them into balls for them to explore.

Homemade Breadsticks

Most people love a breadstick – it's an easy option, works on the go and is fab as a vessel to add extras in via dips and sauces. These are so easy and don't contain any added salt. You can easily experiment with a little more texture and flavour by adding different things to sprinkle on top like sesame seeds, fennel seeds, herbs or even cheese, but they are delicious as they are and make a great alternative to shop-bought breadsticks. They are not too hard, but add some crunch, so you might want to wait until your baby has explored plenty of textures and some harder finger foods before offering these.

Prep: 15 minutes
Cook: 10–15 minutes
Makes: 10–12 breadsticks

180g plain flour, plus extra for dusting
1 tsp baking powder
1 tsp dried oregano
140ml milk of choice
½ tbsp olive oil
handful of seeds (for example, sesame, poppy or fennel) or a sprinkle of my Super Duper Seed Mix (see page 125) (optional)

Switching ingredients in/out: You can use gluten-free flour in this recipe, but the breadsticks come out a little crispier!

Storing leftovers: Will keep in an airtight container for 1 week.

1 Line two baking trays with greaseproof paper and put to one side. Preheat the oven to 220°C/200°C fan.

2 Put the flour, baking powder and oregano into a bowl. Give it a mix to combine, then slowly add the milk, mixing until it forms a dough.

3 Transfer the dough onto a floured surface. Knead the dough for a few minutes to bring it together into a smooth ball. If the dough is a little wet, you can add a little extra flour here, if needed.

4 Using a rolling pin, roll out the dough into a rough rectangle (about 18 x 20cm in size) and then, using a blunt knife, cut it into 12 thin strips (about 2cm wide).

5 Place the strips onto the lined baking tray, stretching them slightly to longer 30-cm lengths. Drizzle with a little oil and brush it all over the breadsticks so they are evenly coated. Sprinkle over the seeds (if using).

6 Bake in the middle of the oven for 10–15 minutes (or until turning a little golden), turning halfway to ensure they are golden all over.

7 Allow to cool before serving.

Serving ideas: These are perfect served with hummus or my red pepper dip (see opposite).

Adaptations for the whole family: Make one tray of breadsticks with some chilli and salt in the mix as well and bake separately. You could always add extra seeds or even grated cheese on top.

Smashed Broccoli Pizza Discs

I love these little pizza discs and had a similar recipe a few years ago on my website. They make mini flat pizzas and you could add all sorts of extra toppings if you want. They don't take long to make and are a snacking favourite in our house. They're also a great way to get little ones eating some extra veggies!

Prep: 10 minutes
Cook: 15–20 minutes
Makes: 8 discs

½ head large broccoli
(about 200g)
3 tbsp tomato puree (or red pepper dip – see page 80)
½ tbsp dried oregano
good handful of cheese (about 40g), grated (mozzarella and Cheddar work really well)
drizzle of olive oil (optional)

1. Preheat the oven to 180°C/200°C fan and line a baking tray with greaseproof paper.

2. Trim the stalk off the broccoli and save for another time. Cut the broccoli into 8 large florets.

3. Bring a saucepan of water to the boil, then add the florets and cook for 3–4 minutes (don't be tempted to overcook them as you don't want them to fall apart when squished). Drain and place on the lined tray. Use the bottom of a mug or glass to gently squash the florets flat, to create a disc shape. You might need to move the mug or glass around a bit to squash it flat.

4. Mix the tomato puree with the oregano, then divide and spread over the surface of the smashed broccoli discs.

5. Sprinkle over the cheese, drizzle with the oil (if using), then pop into the oven for 10–15 minutes (or until golden).

6. Remove from the oven and carefully pop the discs onto a plate to cool a little before serving.

Adaptations for the whole family: These are fab as they are. Serve as a snack or as a side as part of your main meal.

Switching ingredients in/out: It's so easy to swap the broccoli for other veg like cauliflower or potatoes. Use a dairy-free cheese alternative if preferred/needed.

Storing leftovers: Cool to room temperature within 2 hours. Place into an airtight container in the fridge and eat within 2 days. Reheat until piping hot and then allow to cool before serving.

Rice Balls with Veg

This recipe is a little fiddly, but it's honestly so worth it. We love these flavour-packed balls as a little side or snack, and they are a great way for young babies to explore a bit more texture too. You can make them using normal rice, but it's not as easy to get it to stick together. Sticky rice works perfectly though, as does leftover risotto rice.

Prep: 15–20 minutes
Cook: 12–15 minutes
Makes: 8 balls

50g broccoli, stalk removed and finely chopped
40g carrot, peeled and finely grated
125g pre-cooked sticky rice
35g grated mozzarella cheese
1 large free-range egg or 1 chia seed egg (see page 40)
1–2 tbsp olive oil
1–2 heaped tbsp plain flour

Switching ingredients in/out: You can easily switch veggies in or out for this recipe. Use whatever you have that needs using up, but the trick is to chop it all very small!

1 In a bowl, combine the broccoli, carrot, rice, mozzarella and egg (or chia seed egg).

2 Heat 1 tablespoon of the oil in a medium frying pan over a medium heat. Add the rice mix and cook for 5 minutes, stirring occasionally until the egg is cooked or the mixture is browning slightly and the cheese melted.

3 Remove to a bowl to cool for 6–8 minutes, or until you are able to handle the mixture without burning your hands! Keep the pan to one side for later.

4 Carefully form the mixture into 8 balls, squashing it together.

5 Put the flour in a shallow bowl and carefully dust each ball all over with flour. You might need to squidge them back and forth in your hands to help them form a really tight ball again and hold together well.

6 Add a drizzle of oil to the pan, if needed, and gently fry the balls for 3–4 minutes on each side (or until golden).

7 Serve one or two balls on their own to your baby as little finger foods or offer a few balls as a snack for a toddler.

Adaptations for the whole family: These are delicious dipped in a bit of sweet chilli sauce or with a squeeze of lemon on some salad leaves.

Storing leftovers/how to defrost: Cool to room temperature within 1 hour, place into an airtight container in the fridge and eat within 24 hours. Alternatively, place in the freezer and consume within 1 month. Defrost in the fridge overnight or until fully thawed. Reheat until steaming hot all the way through and then allow to cool before serving. Do not reheat rice more than once.

Mini Salmon Nuggets

These super simple little nuggets are a perfect finger food served with a dip or as part of dinner. They contain three different food groups and so are a really nutrient-dense option for babies and offer plenty of flavour too! If you can't use nuts due to allergies, just double the amount of breadcrumbs and omit the almonds.

Prep: 10 minutes
Cook: 12–14 minutes
Makes: 14 nuggets

240g sustainable skinless and boneless salmon fillet, cut into 3–4-cm chunks
50g natural yoghurt, plus extra to serve
½–1 lemon, zested
40g breadcrumbs
40g ground almonds

1 Preheat the oven to 200°C/180°C fan and line a baking sheet with greaseproof paper. Pop the salmon into a bowl with the yoghurt and lemon zest and mix it all around until coated.

2 In another shallow bowl, add the breadcrumbs and ground almonds, mixing it around to combine and leave to one side.

3 Remove the salmon from the yoghurt, shaking off any excess, then roll into the breadcrumb/almond mixture, patting it to coat evenly.

4 Place the nuggets onto the lined tray and bake for 12–14 minutes, or until cooked through and golden. If browning quickly, cover with tin foil and allow time to cook through.

5 Remove to a plate to cool and serve with extra yoghurt, the red pepper dip on page 80 or hummus.

Serving ideas: Serve as part of a larger meal with some peas or veggie sticks, mash or homemade chips (see page 134).

Adaptations for the whole family: Serve with some salad and herby couscous.

Switching ingredients in/out: You can swap the salmon for other fish, chicken or tofu. Leave out the almonds and use plant-based yoghurt if you prefer.

Storing leftovers/how to defrost: Cool to room temperature within 2 hours. Place into an airtight container in the fridge and eat within 2 days. Alternatively, portion into batches and place in the freezer and consume within 3 months. Defrost in the fridge overnight or until fully thawed. Reheat until piping hot and then allow to cool before serving.

Tip: Use premade breadcrumbs or just make your own with a slice of bread (see page 183).

Lentil and Pea Pancakes

These super simple, nutritious pancakes are fab as an on-the-go finger food for your baby and a great way to get iron into a lunch or snack.

Prep: 5 minutes
Cook: 5–6 minutes
Makes: 8–10 pancakes

150g tin cooked green or
   brown lentils, drained well
handful of frozen peas
   (about 40g), fully defrosted
½ tsp smoked paprika
2 tbsp self-raising flour
1 tbsp olive oil

1 Pop the lentils, peas, smoked paprika and 1 tablespoon of water into a blender. Blend until it forms a thick paste, then stir in the flour (you might need a little more if your lentils haven't been drained so well).

2 Heat the oil in a large non-stick frying pan over a medium-high heat.

3 Scoop out 1 tablespoon of the mixture at a time and carefully pop it into the pan, pressing down the top a little to flatten. Cook for 2–3 minutes on each side until golden.

4 Remove to a plate and allow to cool for 10 minutes or so before serving (this allows them to firm up a little).

Serving ideas: These are also great served on the go or as a snack with a little natural yoghurt for dunking.

Adaptations for the whole family: Serve with a herby salad and a little crumbled feta.

Storing leftovers/how to defrost: Cool to room temperature within 2 hours. Place into an airtight container in the fridge and eat within 2 days. Alternatively, place in the freezer with baking paper between each one and consume within 3 months. Defrost in the fridge overnight or until fully thawed. Reheat until piping hot and then allow to cool before serving.

Broccoli Couscous Cakes

I *love* these little couscous cakes – they are so simple and tasty. They can be a little crumbly, but I've experimented with this recipe to get them to hold together enough to pick up. They taste fab and are really great as a soft but experimental texture for babies and toddlers.

Prep: 10 minutes
Cook: 20–25 minutes
Makes: 12 cakes

1 tbsp ground flaxseed
180ml boiling water
180g uncooked couscous (wholegrain, if available)
1 tsp dried oregano
100g frozen (or fresh) broccoli
2 tbsp tomato puree
2 tbsp ground almonds
35g cheese, grated (mozzarella or Cheddar work well)

1. In a small bowl, mix the flaxseed with 2 tablespoons of the boiling water. Give it a mix, then leave to one side.

2. In a medium bowl, add the couscous and oregano. Give it a mix and add the remaining boiling water, then pop a plate on top to cover the bowl and leave for about 5 minutes.

3. Meanwhile, preheat the oven to 200°C/180°C fan and lightly oil a 12-hole cupcake or muffin tin.

4. Once the couscous is cooked, break it up with a fork and put to one side.

5. Bring a small saucepan of water to the boil.

6. Cook the broccoli for around 5 minutes (or around 5–6 minutes if using frozen broccoli), drain and flash under cold water before dicing it into really small pieces. Add it to the couscous along with the tomato puree, ground almonds, grated cheese and flaxseed mix, and give it a good stir, making sure everything is mixed together.

7. Divide the mixture between the 12 cupcake holes, filling each one nearly to the top and pressing down firmly with the back of a spoon to really make the filling compact.

8. Bake in the middle of the oven for 10–15 minutes, or until lightly golden.

9. Remove the cakes from the oven and let them cool completely in the tray. Then, carefully run a blunt knife around the sides of the cakes, lift them out of the tray and serve.

Adaptations for the whole family: These couscous cakes are yummy as they are, though you can mix a little harissa and yoghurt together for a spicy dip to dunk them into.

Storing leftovers: Cool to room temperature within 2 hours. Place into an airtight container in the fridge and eat within 2 days.

Omelette Fingers Three Ways

I always find omelettes such a quick and easy go-to when weaning and feeding little ones, especially Raffy who would *always* munch on an omelette (Ada wasn't as keen on egg initially!). Omelettes can be changed up so easily and make perfect little finger foods, and also go well in a packed lunch too. I love to change up what I pop in them, so here I've given you three ideas to offer a variety for your baby. Feel free to create your own versions too.

Prep: 5 minutes
Cook: 10 minutes
Makes: 16 sticks/fingers

3 large free-range eggs
drizzle of olive oil

For combo 1:
50g chestnut mushrooms,
  finely chopped
1 medium ripe tomato,
  finely chopped
2 sprigs of basil, finely chopped

For combo 2:
25g spinach, washed and
  finely chopped
25g mature Cheddar cheese,
  coarsely grated

For combo 3:
50g red pepper, deseeded
  and finely chopped
5g nutritional yeast

1 Whisk the eggs in a bowl.

2 Heat the oil in a small frying pan over a medium heat.

3 For combo 1, cook the mushrooms for 2–3 minutes stirring occasionally. Then add the tomato, basil and whisked eggs to the pan.

4 For combo 2, add the spinach and cheese to the whisked eggs and mix it all together. Add the mix to the pan.

5 For combo 3, cook the pepper in the pan for 3–4 minutes, stirring occasionally, then add the nutritional yeast and whisked eggs.

6 Move the pan around to cook the egg, breaking up the middle with a wooden spoon so the middle cooks. Then flatten it all out and cook for 3–5 minutes over a medium-low heat, popping a lid on to cook completely.

7 Once the egg is cooked, carefully slide onto a chopping board and cut into fingers. Serve after it has cooled a little (or leave to cool completely).

Adaptations for the whole family: You can add a bit of spice with some freshly sliced red chilli mixed in for adults.

Storing leftovers/how to defrost: Cool to room temperature within 2 hours. Place into an airtight container in the fridge and eat within 2 days. Alternatively, place in the freezer with baking paper between and consume within 3 months. Defrost in the fridge overnight or until fully thawed. Reheat until piping hot and then allow to cool before serving.

Beetroot and Pea Crackers

These delicious and crunchy little crackers are great for babies and toddlers to try. They are so flavourful and are full of nutrients too, with the peas, beetroot and sunflower seeds included. A lovely little on-the-go option!

Prep: 15–20 minutes
Cook: 20–25 minutes
Makes: around 30 crackers

85g vacuum-packed beetroot in natural juices, drained
25g frozen peas, defrosted
1 tbsp sunflower seeds
½ tsp ground cumin
20g Parmesan, grated (optional)
165g plain flour, plus extra for dusting
½ tsp baking powder
15g unsalted butter or dairy-free spread

Switching ingredients in/out: You can easily make these dairy-free by leaving out the cheese or using a vegan alternative and using a plant-based spread.

Adaptations for the whole family: These are delicious as they are, dunked in dips or with some cheese and pickle on top!

1 Preheat the oven to 200°C/180°C fan. Line two large baking trays with greaseproof paper.

2 Add the beetroot, peas, sunflower seeds and cumin to a food processor and blend to create a thick purple mix.

3 Add the Parmesan (if using), flour and baking powder. Slowly pulse until it comes together.

4 Add the butter and pulse to blend, then slowly add 20–30 millilitres of water, a little at a time, pulsing the mix until the dough just comes together (the dough should be coming away from the sides of the bowl and not be sticky).

5 Transfer the dough to a floured surface and roll it around to form a nice ball.

6 Using a rolling pin, roll out the dough until it is around ½cm thick and cut using whatever cutters you fancy (round shapes are good for younger babies as they don't have the crispy corners) or just cut with a knife into 4-cm wide squares. Place the crackers onto the lined trays, spaced 1cm apart. Prick each with a fork a couple of times.

7 Bake in the middle of the oven for 20–25 minutes, or until the edges start to brown.

8 Leave to cool on the trays for 5 minutes, then remove to a cooling rack to cool completely.

9 Serve as they are or with a simple dip.

Storing leftovers/how to defrost: Cool to room temperature within 2 hours. Place into an airtight container in the fridge and eat within 2 days. Alternatively, place in the freezer and consume within 2 months. Defrost in the fridge overnight or until fully thawed.

Image overleaf →

Turkey and Mushroom Meatballs

These super simple meatballs are made with extra veggies and contain lots of flavours! They work really well as little finger foods for babies or can be added to a pasta sauce for some extra flavour and nutrients.

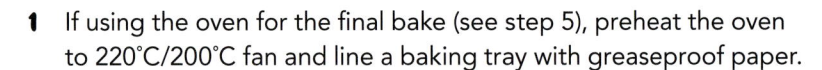

Prep: 10 minutes
Cook: 16 minutes
Makes: 12 meatballs

½ tbsp olive oil (plus an extra drizzle for cooking the meatballs)
130g chestnut mushrooms, finely chopped
2 sprigs of basil, leaves removed, stalks and leaves finely chopped
¼ tsp ground cinnamon
200g turkey mince

1   If using the oven for the final bake (see step 5), preheat the oven to 220°C/200°C fan and line a baking tray with greaseproof paper.

2   Heat the oil in a medium frying pan over a medium heat. Add the mushrooms and basil stalks and cook for 5 minutes, stirring occasionally until the liquid from the mushrooms has evaporated.

3   Add the ground cinnamon and cook for a further minute.

4   Remove to a bowl and leave to cool. Once cooled, stir in the turkey mince and add the basil leaves. Give it a good mix, then form into 12 balls.

5   If baking in the oven, pop the meatballs onto the lined tray, drizzle with a little oil and bake in the middle of the oven for 10 minutes, or until cooked through. If frying, heat a drizzle of oil in the frying pan over a medium heat, add the meatballs and fry for 8–10 minutes, moving them around to ensure they are golden on each side.

6   Serve warm on their own as finger foods or a snack, or as part of a meal.

Serving ideas: Offer as a snack with veggie sticks or on pasta with some sauce.

Adaptations for the whole family: Add some extra spices or finely grated mozzarella into the mix.

Storing leftovers/how to defrost: Cool to room temperature within 2 hours. Place into an airtight container in the fridge and eat within 2 days. Alternatively, place in the freezer and consume within 3 months. Defrost in the fridge overnight or until fully thawed. Reheat until piping hot and then allow to cool before serving.

Smashed and Roasted Chickpeas

Whole chickpeas can be a bit of a choking hazard for young babies and toddlers, so I've created a twist on the classic roast chickpeas recipe by smashing them at the end. You don't have to completely flatten the chickpeas, so gently squashing is fine, but just make sure any that you give to your baby are not whole round chickpeas. These are super moreish and a great source of nutrients, as well as a fab new texture for older babies and toddlers to explore.

Prep: 5 minutes
Cook: 15 minutes
Makes: 400g

400g tin chickpeas, drained
   and rinsed
½ tsp ground coriander
1 tsp smoked paprika
good drizzle of olive oil

1   Preheat the oven to 220°C/200°C fan. Pour the chickpeas into a roasting tray and pat them down with a clean tea towel to dry them.

2   Sprinkle over the coriander, paprika and olive oil, and give the tray a good shake to coat the chickpeas.

3   Bake in the middle of the oven for 15 minutes until golden and crispy.

4   Remove from the oven and carefully smash the chickpeas with a potato masher or press down gently with a glass to ensure they aren't whole, making them flat and easily 'grabbable' for babies before serving.

Adaptations for the whole family: These can be eaten as a snack but also sprinkled on top of salads or soups, or served in sandwiches. Leave half the tray un-squashed if you prefer to eat them whole!

Switching ingredients in/out: Feel free to add whatever flavours work for you, or simply increase the coriander and paprika.

Storing leftovers: Cool to room temperature within 2 hours. Place into an airtight container in the fridge and eat within 2 days.

 Tip: These are ideal for slightly older babies (from around 9 months) and will give them plenty of practice using their index finger and thumb (pincer grip style) to start self-feeding.

Avocado and Raspberry Muffins

This muffin recipe is a bit different as it really packs in the nutrients and includes healthy fats and three different fruits. I've added avocado as it is such a nutrient-dense food. If you open your avocado and it's under-/overripe (which always happens, right?), you can easily replace it with one small, well-mashed pear – it works just as well and adds extra sweetness. You can even use frozen avocado if you have it – just make sure it's defrosted first.

Prep: 10 minutes
Cook: 18–20 minutes
Makes: 10–12 muffins

1 large banana (about 110g)
½ ripe avocado or 1 small pear, well mashed
50ml milk of choice (leave out if using pear instead of the avocado)
1 large free-range egg or 1 chia seed egg (see page 40)
50ml olive oil
150g self-raising flour
large handful of raspberries (about 70g), plus extra for topping

1 Preheat the oven to 210°C/190°C fan. Line a 12-hole cupcake or muffin tin with cases.

2 In a large bowl, add the banana and avocado or pear and mash together really well.

3 Add the milk (if using) and egg and give it a good whisk together until it gets a little bubbly.

4 Add the oil and flour and stir through, mixing really well and adding a splash more milk if the mixture feels stiff.

5 Add the raspberries and stir them through, breaking them up a little as you do so.

6 Give it all a good mix then divide it between the 12 cases. Pop a few extra raspberries on top of some of the muffins to add some extra colour and fruitiness.

7 Bake in the middle of the oven for around 18 minutes, or until golden and risen.

8 Leave to cool in the tin for 5 minutes, then remove to a cooling rack. The muffins may need a few minutes to solidify. Serve warm or cold.

Switching ingredients in/out: Switch the raspberries for blueberries.

Storing leftovers/how to defrost: Cool to room temperature within 2 hours. Place into an airtight container in the fridge and eat within 2 days. Alternatively, place in the freezer with baking paper between and consume within 3 months. Defrost in the fridge overnight or until fully thawed.

Adaptations for the whole family: Throw in some white chocolate chips to make these a little like shop-bought raspberry and white chocolate muffins (my favourite) or enjoy as they are with a cup of tea.

Frozen Banana Bites

These are such a tasty snack option and contain two out of three of the main food groups, making them a super simple balanced snack. This recipe is also a great way of using up those sad looking bananas and not letting them go to waste! I've used my Super Duper Seed Mix to sprinkle on top, but, for older kids, you can experiment with chocolate chips or colourful sprinkles if you prefer. They are very sweet as they are though, so don't need huge amounts of extra sweetness.

Prep: 5 minutes, plus 2½ hours freezing time
Makes: 5–7 bites

2 ripe bananas, peeled
around 150g thick Greek yoghurt or dairy-free alternative
1–2 tbsp milled seeds or my Super Duper Seed Mix (see page 125)

1 Mash the bananas in a bowl. Line a tray or plate that will fit in your freezer with greaseproof paper.

2 Dollop on heaped tablespoons of the mashed banana, creating 5–7 little circular 'bites', about 5cm wide. Pop in the freezer for 1½ hours, keeping the tray as flat as possible.

3 Remove from the freezer and roughly spread some of the yoghurt on top. Sprinkle with the seeds and pop back in the freezer for 1 hour to set fully.

4 Take the bites out of the freezer 5–10 minutes before you want to serve them. You can use a fork to hold the bites if they are getting too messy/cold!

Adaptations for the whole family: Experiment with different toppings. Drizzle the bites with peanut butter or melted chocolate, or add in chocolate chips for older kids.

Switching ingredients in/out: Use plant-based yoghurt if you prefer or need to.

Storing leftovers: These will keep in the freezer for around 3 months.

Tip: Like ice lollies, these might be a little cold for some babies to handle, so may be better as a snack for older toddlers.

Polenta Sticks and Dip

I think polenta is an underused food for babies. It's super soft and squidges nicely between fingers and thumb, but makes a nice solid shape when baked – so is ideal as a finger food. These little 'chips' make a fab vessel for a dip and are a great way for your baby to explore new flavours by experimenting with toppings.

Prep: 10 minutes, plus cooling
Cook: 25–30 minutes
Makes: 16 sticks

500ml low-salt vegetable stock or water
125g polenta, plus 2 tbsp extra for dusting
15g cheese (for example, Cheddar or Parmesan), finely grated (optional)
1½ tbsp olive oil

For the dip:
½ ripe avocado (about 100g)
2 sprigs of mint, leaves picked
150g tinned chickpeas, drained and rinsed
juice of ½ lemon

Adaptations for the whole family: Polenta doesn't offer much of a flavour kick, though using low-salt stock and adding the cheese will help. You can also add a variety of toppings when popping them in the oven, such as paprika, cumin, other cheeses, garlic powder or cumin seeds. The sticks are delicious with the dip though, whatever your age.

1 Line a 24 x 14cm loaf tin with greaseproof paper.

2 Bring a medium saucepan of stock or water to the boil, then turn down to a simmer. Over a medium heat, whisk in the polenta and keep whisking until it starts to thicken – this should only take a minute.

3 Once all the stock or water is absorbed, remove the pan from the heat and stir in the cheese (if using).

4 Pour the mixture into the lined tin so it is around 1–2cm thick and spread out evenly. Don't worry – the mix isn't meant to fill the tin to the top. Leave to cool and set. You can speed this up by popping it in the fridge for 30 minutes.

5 Meanwhile, preheat the oven to 220°C/200°C fan and line a baking tray with greaseproof paper.

6 Once the polenta is set, carefully tip it out of the tin onto a chopping board and cut into 16 sticks. Pop the sticks onto the lined tray and sprinkle with the extra polenta to add a crispy edge. Drizzle with oil and bake in the middle of the oven for 20–25 minutes, or until golden.

7 While the polenta sticks are baking, make the dip by popping all the ingredients into a blender with 1–2 tablespoons of water and blend until it forms a nice thick dip. Add a splash more water if you want it to be thinner.

8 Serve the dip alongside the polenta sticks.

Storing leftovers/how to defrost: Cool to room temperature within 2 hours. Place into an airtight container in the fridge and eat within 2 days. Alternatively, place in the freezer with baking paper between and consume within 3 months. Defrost in the fridge overnight or until fully thawed. Reheat in the oven until piping hot and then allow to cool before serving. The dip will keep in the fridge in an airtight container for 1–2 days.

Raisin and Banana Bars

These are great alternatives to the little packet bars that my kids love as an on-the-go snack, but here the sweetness comes from the fruits and veggies and not table sugar! They are such a winner and are even an alternative to cakes at parties too. I make them in silicone mini loaf trays.

Prep: 10 minutes
Cook: 20–25 minutes
Makes: 12 mini 'loaves' or cakes

200g raisins (or sultanas)
2 tbsp boiling water
1 ripe banana (about 100g), peeled
75ml vegetable oil
2 tbsp milk of choice
200g self-raising flour
2 tbsp ground almonds

1 Preheat the oven 200°C/180°C fan. Line a 12-hole mini loaf tin or a 12-hole cupcake or muffin tin with cases.

2 Pop the raisins or sultanas into a food processor with the boiling water and give it a whizz to chop it up really well.

3 Add the banana, oil and milk, and give it another whizz.

4 Pop in the flour and almonds and give it a pulse. Check it is all mixed in then divide the mixture between the cases.

5 Bake in the middle of the oven for around 20–25 minutes (or until cooked through and golden).

6 Leave to cool in the tin for 5 minutes, then remove to a cooling rack before serving.

Adaptations for the whole family: These are fairly sweet, so are perfect as they are. They are also great for breakfast with a little yoghurt dolloped on the side.

Switching ingredients in/out: You can swap the raisins for other dried fruits really easily. Leave out the almonds if needed.

Storing leftovers/how to defrost: Cool to room temperature within 2 hours. Place into an airtight container in the fridge and eat within 2 days. Alternatively, place in the freezer and consume within 3 months. Defrost in the fridge overnight or until fully thawed.

Veggie Cornmeal Squares

I did a similar recipe to this in *How to Feed Your Toddler* and it went down a treat. This is super easy and makes a lovely bread that works well on its own or even cut into finger sticks and dipped into soup. It packs in lots of veggies too, so is a really nutritious option and a fab on-the-go snack. Make sure you chop the veggies really well if needed and give the sweetcorn a little blend to ensure the kernels aren't whole for younger babies who are just exploring textures.

Prep: 10 minutes
Cook: 30–35 minutes
Makes: 12 squares/1 loaf

200g self-raising flour
1 large free-range egg
200ml milk of choice
60g cornmeal or polenta
60g mature Cheddar cheese, grated
150g cauliflower, finely chopped
100g tinned sweetcorn, drained, blitzed a little for younger kids
1 large carrot (about 100g), peeled and grated
a few chives, finely chopped

1 Preheat the oven to 200°C/180°C fan. Line a 20cm square ovenproof tin with greaseproof paper.

2 Sift the flour into a large bowl and make a well in the middle. Add in the egg and milk, and combine with a whisk to get rid of any lumps. Add the cornmeal (or polenta), cheese and all the veg, and mix together thoroughly. Sprinkle in the chives and give it one last mix.

3 Add the mixture to the lined tin. Bake in the middle of the oven for 30–35 minutes, or until golden brown.

4 Leave to cool in the tin for 5 minutes, then remove to a cooling rack and leave to cool for 10–15 minutes.

5 Cut into 12 squares and serve with my Tomato Soup (see page 150) or as a side to a hearty recipe like my Mixed Bean Casserole (see page 174) or with the red pepper dip on page 80.

Adaptations for the whole family: These are fab as they are for everyone. Cut into finger shapes for little babies or squares for older toddlers and adults.

Storing leftovers/how to defrost: Cool to room temperature within 2 hours. Place into an airtight container in the fridge and eat within 2 days. Alternatively, place in the freezer and consume within 3 months. Defrost in the fridge overnight or until fully thawed. Reheat until piping hot and then allow to cool before serving.

Cocoa Oat Cookies

These cookies aren't super sweet, but they are great for babies and toddlers – nice and soft on the inside and a little crisp on the outside. I don't use cocoa much as it contains caffeine naturally, which isn't ideal for little ones, but a little (like in this recipe) will be fine. These lovely, simple little biscuits are full of lots of nutrients and are a hit with my two (and me!).

Prep: 5 minutes
Cook: 10–12 minutes
Makes: 8–10 cookies

1 ripe banana (about 100g), peeled and mashed
2 tbsp smooth peanut butter
2 tbsp ground flaxseed
1 tsp cocoa powder
10g unsalted butter, softened, or plant-based spread
50g porridge oats

1 Preheat the oven to 200°C/180°C fan. Line a large baking tray with greaseproof paper.

2 In a bowl, add the banana, peanut butter, ground flaxseed, cocoa powder, butter and oats. Give it a good mix.

3 Dollop heaped tablespoons of the cookie mix onto the lined tray, creating 8–10 biscuits. Press down the cookies so they are around 5cm wide and ½cm thick.

4 Bake in the middle of the oven for 10–12 minutes until golden and cooked through. Leave to cool a little on the tray, then remove to a cooling rack.

5 Serve warm or on the go.

Adaptations for the whole family: These are delicious as they are, but if you want a sweet kick you could drizzle some melted chocolate on top or throw in some chocolate chips to your version. Double up the recipe if you're making them for a lot of people.

Storing leftovers: Will keep in an airtight container for 2 days or in the freezer for about 3 months.

Image overleaf →

Plum and Banana Teething Biscuit

These simple little biscuits are so easy to make. Younger babies who are used to a variety of finger foods can gum the edges of these easily as they are fairly soft and, for older kids, they make a nice dunking biscuit. They contain no added sugar and just the sweetness from the fruits, and are great for adults with a cup of tea too! I find these super moreish. You will make plenty with this recipe and they are ideal to freeze for another day.

Prep: 5 minutes
Cook: 10–12 minutes
Makes: 20–30 biscuits

1 large ripe banana (about 120g), peeled and mashed
1 ripe plum (about 40g), destoned, finely chopped and mashed
100g plain flour (plus up to 50g extra and a little for dusting)
30g porridge oats
30g unsalted butter, softened, or plant-based spread
zest of ½ orange

Switching ingredients in/out: You can use 1 finely chopped and mashed fig instead of the plum.

1 Line a large baking sheet with greaseproof paper and preheat the oven to 220°C/200°C fan.

2 In a bowl, combine the banana and plum.

3 Add the flour, oats, butter and orange zest and mix until it forms a ball of dough. (At this stage, you might need to add up to 50g more flour, depending on how ripe and juicy your plum is.)

4 Transfer the dough to a floured surface. Using a rolling pin, roll out the dough until it is 1cm thick (making them thicker like this means they are a little softer inside and so easier for babies to munch; you can roll the dough more thinly for older children to offer a harder biscuit).

5 Cut out the biscuits using a glass or cutter. Depending on the thickness and size of your cutter you should get around 20–30 biscuits.

6 Pop the biscuits onto the lined tray and bake in the middle of the oven for 10–12 minutes, or until starting to turn golden.

7 Leave to cool for 5 minutes on the tray, then remove to a cooling rack.

Adaptations for the whole family: Once the dough is rolled out, add a handful of chopped cranberries or other dried fruits to add a little extra sweetness. This works for older toddlers too. Alternatively, dust the biscuits with a little icing sugar after baking. You can also use yoghurt with mixed fruit or my chia seed jam (see page 117) as a dip for older children.

Storing leftovers/how to defrost: Will keep in an airtight container in the fridge for 2 days or in the freezer for 2–3 months. Defrost in the fridge overnight before eating.

Breakfasts

We're big breakfast eaters in our house. My kids love a good breakfast and I definitely find that they've got used to having plenty of variety in the morning, which keeps me on my toes.

Once babies are familiar with foods and have had their first meals, they can start having shop-bought breakfast cereals – go with the no added sugar and fortified versions – but I wouldn't make them everyday options. It's good to vary what you offer to babies and toddlers so they don't get bored with the same brekkie every day. If your baby suddenly refuses a firm favourite, it can make the mornings a bit tricky.

A lot of the breakfasts I like to make are ones that can be made ahead, frozen and then heated up ready for a quick morning meal, such as breakfast muffins, pancakes, bakes and bars. There are plenty of those kinds of brekkies in this section, so I hope you enjoy them too.

When your baby is little, an omelette strip or two, some yoghurt and fruit or some toast and topping are all good options, but if you're looking for variety, I've got some great ideas in this section.

Lots of these recipes are 'on-the-go' options too. I used to love eating like this with Raffy when he was little and weaning, so I've created quite a few of these recipes so they are easy to eat out and about or take to a friend's house.

I really hope you enjoy these recipes.

Eggy Avo Toast

Eggy bread/French toast is such an easy way to get some extra nutrients in at breakfast. I love making it with avocado as something a bit different for the family for breakfast. This works for lunch or snacks too, of course. The added flavours here give a little extra kick. You can make this into an open toastie or squash a second slice on top of the avocado to make a proper toastie. You can also cut it into sticks or squares for babies or toddlers to nibble on. This one's best for babies who have had plenty of experience with finger foods and toast sticks!

Prep: 10 minutes
Cook: 6–8 minutes
Serves: 1 adult and
1–2 babies/toddlers

1–2 large free-range eggs
¼ tsp smoked paprika, plus
   extra for sprinkling
1 tbsp olive oil
2 slices of good-quality bread
   (wholemeal if possible)
1 ripe avocado, peeled and
   destoned
a squeeze of lemon or lime

1   In a shallow bowl, crack the eggs, whisk and then add the paprika.

2   Heat the oil in a medium frying pan over a high heat.

3   Dip the bread slices into the egg mix and hold them up to let the excess egg drip off.

4   Add the bread to the pan and fry for 2–3 minutes, or until golden and cooked. Flip and repeat on the other side. If you have any leftover egg mix, just fry it off with the eggy bread (or keep dunking more bread). The type of bread you use will depend on how much mix it soaks up so it can vary each time.

5   While the bread is frying, mash up the avocado with a little lemon or lime juice.

6   Serve cut into lengths for younger babies with the mashed avocado on top or offered as a toastie half for older toddlers with the avocado in the middle and a sprinkle more paprika.

Adaptations for the whole family: This is great as it is served as a toastie. Add some crumbled feta with the avocado too, if you like.

Storing leftovers/how to defrost (eggy bread, without avocado): Cool the eggy bread to room temperature within 2 hours. Place into an airtight container in the fridge with baking paper between the layers and eat within 2 days. Alternatively, place in the freezer and consume within 3 months. Reheat straight from freezer in the oven until piping hot and then allow to cool before serving.

Traffic Light Pancakes

This is a slightly longer recipe, but it makes a big batch of varied, colourful and exciting pancakes for the whole family. It's so handy to batch-cook pancakes, pop them in the freezer and then defrost them overnight and heat through for brekkie the next day. Pancakes were a staple in our house when Raffy was weaning, and he still loves them to this day.

Prep: 10–15 minutes
Cook: 15–20 minutes
Makes: 15–20 pancakes
(500g batch of mix)

For the batter:
1 medium banana, peeled and mashed
1 large free-range egg or 1 chia seed egg (see page 40)
120g self-raising flour, plus 1 extra tbsp for the raspberry flavour
170ml milk of choice
1 tbsp milled seeds
1 tbsp olive oil

For the flavours:
100g raspberries, roughly mashed
50g finely grated carrot
zest of 1 orange
30g spinach, washed and dried

Tip: If you prefer, you can just make the mix one colour, which takes a little less time and equipment (though it's not as exciting for little ones!).

1 In a large bowl, add the banana, egg (or chia seed egg), flour, milk and seeds, and give it a good mix to combine.

2 Divide the mix roughly into three bowls (about 160g in each bowl).

3 Mash the raspberries into one batch, adding the extra tablespoon of flour as this mix is usually looser due to the liquid content of the fruit, and put to one side.

4 Mix the grated carrot and zest of the orange into the second batch and pop to one side.

5 For the final batch, add the spinach and remaining mix to a blender and whizz (this will ensure the spinach really breaks down and gives you a fab green colour).

6 You should now have three different colour mixes!

7 To cook, heat the oil in a large non-stick frying pan over a medium heat and roll it around so the pan is covered with a thin layer (this will stop the pancakes sticking and help cook them nicely). Put a heaped tablespoon of each batter (making 6-cm wide pancakes) into the pan and cook for 4 minutes, until the edges of the pancakes have started to solidify. Flip and cook the other side until firm and cooked through. Pop the cooked pancakes on a warm plate and continue until you use up all the batter.

8 Serve immediately just as they are. These are also great for on the go!

Serving ideas: You can top these with a dollop of thick yoghurt and extra fruit.

Storing leftovers/how to defrost: The cooked pancakes will keep in the fridge for 2 days in an airtight container with baking paper between each one, or in the freezer for around 3–6 months. Thoroughly defrost in the fridge overnight. If serving warm, heat through until piping hot and then allow to cool before serving.

Overnight Coconut Pud

I have to confess that my kids aren't so keen on 'cold porridge', as they call it, but it's such an easy and delicious breakfast. If you introduce this kind of brekkie early on, it's much more likely that it'll be accepted (we definitely focused on hot porridge far too much in this house!) – it's the best feeling when you have something ready for the kids to eat as soon as you wake up! Raffy has this heated and loves it and Ada likes it with a *lot* of coconut and strawberries on top. This is also a fab one for building on textures – everything is super soft, but it includes plenty of bumpy textures for your little one to explore.

Prep: 10 minutes
(plus overnight soaking)
Serves: 1 adult and
2 babies/toddlers

100g porridge oats
250ml milk of choice, plus extra
   to loosen
4 tbsp coconut (or Greek)
   yoghurt, plus extra to serve
1 tbsp chia seeds
1 small apple, cored and grated
1 tbsp desiccated coconut, plus
   a little extra to serve
a few strawberries, hulled and
   sliced
a sprinkle of poppy seeds
   (optional)

1 Pop the oats, milk, yoghurt and chia seeds into a container with a lid. Give it a stir, then stir in the apple and desiccated coconut. Give it another good stir, pop the lid on and leave in the fridge for a few hours or overnight.

2 Before serving, add a good splash of milk and give it a stir to loosen. Divide into bowls and serve with an extra dollop of coconut yoghurt, sliced strawberries and a sprinkle of desiccated coconut and poppy seeds (if using) on top.

Adaptations for the whole family: This one is really delicious for the whole family as it is. Add plenty of chopped strawberries on top for older children and adults.

Storing leftovers: Place into an airtight container in the fridge and eat within 2 days.

Tip: This is a great one to make ahead – if you make a big batch, it might last you for a couple of days.

Easy On-the-Go Brekkie Bars

I know that sometimes the chewy bars you get from the shops can be simple options for babies and toddlers, so I wanted to make my own version that you can make in bulk, pop in the freezer and get out as and when you need them for an on-the-go breakfast or snack! These are so delicious and contain plenty of nutrients and flavours too.

Prep: 10 minutes
Cook: 10–12 minutes
Makes: 12 bars

8 dried dates (Medjool if possible; about 100g), destoned
boiling water to cover the dates
80g porridge oats
1 medium apple, cored and coarsely grated
1 tsp ground cinnamon
1 heaped tbsp ground almonds

1 Pop the dates into a bowl and cover with the boiling water. Leave to one side for 5 minutes then drain.

2 Preheat the oven to 210°C/190°C fan. Line a 20cm square baking tin with greaseproof paper.

3 In a food processor, add the oats, apple, cinnamon, ground almonds and drained, soaked dates. Pulse the mix until it forms a sticky paste, then remove to the baking tin.

4 Spread it out to make an even layer using the back of a spoon dunked in warm water (this helps to spread it without it sticking!).

5 Bake in the middle of the oven for 10–12 minutes, or until golden and cooked.

6 Remove from the tin and, while still slightly warm, cut into 12 bars and then leave to cool completely.

7 Serve on their own, as they are.

Adaptation for the whole family: These are lovely enjoyed with a cup of tea or as an on-the-go snack for you.

Switching ingredients in/out: Swap the dates for other dried fruits if you prefer.

Storing leftovers/how to defrost: Place into an airtight container in the fridge with baking paper between layers and eat within 2 days. Alternatively, place in the freezer and consume within 3 months. Place in the fridge to defrost overnight or until fully thawed.

Mango and Raspberry Breakfast Bake

I love doing these porridgy, oaty bakes for my kids as they work in so many ways and are really nutritious and filling. This is similar to the Blueberry Baked Oats in *How to Feed Your Toddler*, but I've changed it up a bit and I love the combination of ingredients here. It's my favourite served warm with some yoghurt.

Prep: 10 minutes
Cook: 25–30 minutes
Makes: 10 bars or, as a bake, serves 2 adults and 2 babies/toddlers, with leftovers

2 tbsp chia seeds
5 tbsp hot water
160g porridge oats
30g blended seeds/nuts
  (you can use the Super Duper
  Seed Mix on page 125)
pinch–½ tsp ground ginger
40g self-raising flour
100g frozen mango, defrosted
  and well chopped
100ml milk of choice
100g frozen raspberries,
  defrosted (or fresh)

For the chia seed jam:
2 tsp chia seeds
125g frozen raspberries,
  defrosted and mashed
  (or fresh)

1. In a small bowl, mix the chia seeds with the water and leave to one side.

2. Preheat the oven to 200°C/180°C fan. Line a 20cm square ovenproof tin with greaseproof paper.

3. Pop the oats, seeds/nuts ginger and flour in a bowl and stir to combine.

4. Add the mango and milk and stir into the mix. Add the raspberries, roughly mashing them as you go. Stir in the chia seed mix and combine.

5. Tip the mixture into the lined tin, spreading it around so it is even and smooth on top. Bake in the middle of the oven for 25–30 minutes until golden and cooked.

6. Meanwhile, to make the topping, add the chia seeds and mashed raspberries to a small saucepan along with a couple of splashes of water. Cook over a medium heat, stirring until combined and thickened.

7. To serve, either scoop out the bake while it is warm and gooey and serve with some yoghurt or topped with a dollop of the chia seed jam, or spread the jam on top, leave to cool and cut into bars for an on-the-go brekkie.

Adaptations for the whole family: This is perfect as is, but if you like foods a little sweeter, add a drizzle of honey on top of your portion.

Storing leftovers/how to defrost: This will keep in the fridge for 2 days in an airtight container, or in the freezer for up to 4 months. Thoroughly defrost in the fridge overnight. Serve cold or heat through until piping hot and then allow to cool before serving.

Image overleaf →

Porridge Four Ways

One of my favourite things about porridge is that it's so versatile. You can make any combination you like – sometimes we add carrot, courgette or beetroot to ours. The tried-and-tested flavours in this recipe work really well, and my kids love them all, but feel free to adapt them. When offering your baby porridge for the first time, you might want to start with it plain and blend the oats a bit first, but you will need less milk if you do this. Because in this recipe it's cooked slowly, it is super soft and easy to eat, even as an early meal for a young baby. You can use baby's normal milk or whatever works for you.

Prep: 5 minutes
Cook: 8–10 minutes
Serves: 1 adult and 1 baby/toddler, with leftovers

For the porridge:
75g porridge oats
280ml milk of choice

For combo 1:
45g (¼ small) sweet potato, peeled and coarsely grated
1 medium pear, coarsely grated
1 tbsp sultanas (finely chopped for babies)

For combo 2:
80g frozen or fresh mixed berries (for example, raspberries, blueberries, strawberries, blackberries)
pinch–¼ tsp ground ginger

For combo 3:
1 medium apple, cored and coarsely grated
good grating of nutmeg or small pinch of ground nutmeg, plus a little extra to serve
1 heaped tbsp per serving of yoghurt of choice

1 To make your basic porridge, add the oats and milk into a medium saucepan (along with the relevant flavour combo, if using – see step 2, 3 or 4). Cook over a medium heat for 8–10 minutes until combined and thickened, stirring occasionally.

2 For combo 1, add the sweet potato and pear to the pan with the oats and milk, then stir in most of the sultanas before heating. Serve sprinkled with the remaining sultanas (finely chopped for babies).

3 For combo 2, add the berries and ginger to the pan with the oats and milk before heating. Go easy on the ginger if your baby hasn't had it before. Serve with a few reserved berries to finish. Give the berries a bit of a mash with a fork after cooking/before serving if needed.

4 For combo 3, add the apple and nutmeg to the pan with the oats and milk before heating. Serve with a dollop of yoghurt and a bit of extra nutmeg.

Serving ideas: Serve with a few fruity finger foods, if you have them. You can also sprinkle on a little Super Duper Seed Mix (see page 125) to add extra nutrients.

Adaptations for the whole family: Add whatever toppings you fancy! You might want to add a pinch more flavours to yours and/or a drizzle of honey on top, depending on your preferences.

Storing leftovers: Cool the porridge to room temperature within 2 hours. Place into an airtight container in the fridge and eat within 2 days. Reheat until piping hot and then allow to cool before serving.

Mini Veggie breakfast

O

My kids and I love going out for a full English, so I wanted to create a mini, simpler version you can make at home. I've made a vegetarian one here with lots of veggies, which are simply topped with some scrambled egg. It's tasty and a great way of getting your little one to have veggies for breakfast too! Depending on your baby's age, this one may need to be really well chopped and offered on a spoon or mashed together when it comes out. It might be better for babies with a little more experience with textures.

Prep: 8 minutes
Cook: 15–20 minutes
Serves: 1 adult and
1–2 babies/toddlers

6 chestnut mushrooms,
    thinly sliced
1 garlic clove, peeled and
    crushed
8 ripe cherry tomatoes,
    roughly chopped
2 tbsp olive oil
6 tbsp tinned butter/kidney
    beans, drained and rinsed
good handful of spinach leaves,
    washed and finely chopped
2–3 large free-range eggs
    (1 per person) or 200g firm
    tofu, crumbled

1 Preheat the grill to high.

2 Pop the mushrooms, garlic and tomatoes into an ovenproof dish. Drizzle with 1 tablespoon of the oil and mix to coat. Grill for 8–10 minutes, or until starting to get golden. Carefully remove from the grill and add the beans and the spinach. Give it a mix, mashing the beans well as you go. Pop back under the grill and cook for 2–3 minutes.

3 Meanwhile, crack the eggs in a bowl and whisk until combined.

4 Heat the remaining oil in a small frying pan over a low-medium heat, add the whisked eggs and cook for 5 minutes, stirring occasionally. If using tofu, crumble into the frying pan and cook for 5 minutes until crispy and golden.

5 Divide the eggs (or tofu) and the veggie mixture between plates and serve.

Adaptation for adults: Serve with half an avocado and some smoky chilli sauce.

Storing leftovers: Cool to room temperature within 2 hours. Place into an airtight container in the fridge and eat within 2 days. Reheat until piping hot and then allow to cool before serving.

Burrito Breakfast Wrap

I love really unique breakfasts and always try to include at least one in the recipe sections of my book. This is a really fab little take on an omelette, where you add it to a wrap with some extras as a super veggie breakfast option! I love it. For younger babies you can just serve sticks of the omelette with some avocado finger foods and then use the wraps for older kids/adults, but it's super tasty, and packs in lots of veggies in the morning too!

Prep: 5 minutes
Cook: 8–10 minutes
Serves: 1 adult and 1 baby/toddler

3 large free-range eggs, whisked
2 heaped tbsp grated mature Cheddar cheese (about 20g)
2 tbsp tinned black beans, drained and rinsed (mashed slightly for younger babies)
½ tbsp olive oil
2 spring onions, peeled, trimmed and thinly sliced
2 sprigs of coriander, leaves and stalks separated and finely chopped
very small handful of baby spinach leaves (about 5–10g), washed and chopped well
2–4 mini (or 2 large) tortilla wraps
½ ripe avocado, peeled, destoned and mashed
a few small tomatoes, finely diced

Tip: Great to have on the go – cut into little rolled up strips.

1. In a bowl, add the eggs, cheese and black beans. Mix to break up the eggs and combine everything, then leave to one side.

2. Heat the oil in a small frying pan over a medium heat. Add the spring onions and coriander stalks and cook for a minute or so, stirring to make sure they don't catch.

3. Add the egg mix to the pan and spread the mix out as flat as you can and continue cooking for around 1 minute.

4. Sprinkle over the spinach and then leave to cook for 3 minutes (or until the egg is fully cooked).

5. Once the egg mix is cooked, remove it to a chopping board.

6. Slice the omelette into thin strips and lay a few strips on each wrap, with a dollop of avocado and some of the chopped coriander and tomatoes on top. Roll up the wrap tightly and squash it down a little before serving. You might want to chop it into little rounds or in half to serve to toddlers, or for younger babies just offer strips of omelette with some mashed avocado as a dip.

Adaptation for adults: Add some hot sauce in your wrap for a bit of spice!

Storing leftovers/how to defrost (omelette strips only): Cool the omelette strips to room temperature within 2 hours. Place into an airtight container in the fridge and eat within 2 days. Alternatively, place in the freezer and consume within 3 months. Defrost in the fridge overnight or until fully thawed. Reheat until piping hot and then allow to cool before serving. Can be eaten cold or hot.

Charlotte's Super Duper Seed Mix with Stewed Fruit

 Ve

I love milled seeds so much – they're such a great way of adding extra flavour and *lots* of extra nutrients to meals. So I wanted to create a new Super Duper Seed Mix that is versatile and goes well with most breakfasts, but can be used with other foods and in baking too. It's one of my fave recipes in the whole book – try sprinkling it on salads, stirring it into soups, popping it on porridge, cereals or yoghurt, adding it to smoothies or mixing it in with crumble toppings. You can leave out the fruity bits if you want to use it on more savoury foods. This recipe makes a batch of stewed fruit too – make sure the fruit is well mashed for younger babies.

Prep: 10 minutes
Cook: 8–10 minutes
Makes: 1 x 750ml jar of Super Duper Seed Mix plus 6 portions of stewed fruit

For the stewed fruit:
300g plums (about 4 medium), destoned and cut into wedges
200g pears (about 2 medium), cored and roughly chopped
juice of 1 large orange and zest of ½
yoghurt of choice, to serve

For the super duper seed mix:
200g mixed nuts (such as almond, pistachio, walnut)
100g mixed seeds (such as pumpkin, sunflower, poppy, linseed)
50g dried or freeze-dried fruit (such as cranberries, raspberries, mango, strawberries)

1 To make the stewed fruit, add the plums, pears, orange juice and zest to a medium saucepan. Bring to the boil, then turn down to a simmer and pop the lid on. Cook for 8–10 minutes until the fruit is soft and has broken down. Stir and then leave to one side.

2 To make the Super Duper Seed Mix, sterilise a 750ml jar. Place the nuts in a food processor and blend to a semi fine powder (stopping regularly to check so it doesn't turn to a paste!), then add the seeds and keep blending/pulsing until it forms a fine powder.

3 If using, add in the dried fruit and pulse to chop up and combine. Check the fruit has been cut up thoroughly (you just want tiny pieces), then pop the whole mix into the sterilised jar.

4 To serve, pop some yoghurt in a bowl with a few tablespoons of the stewed fruit, then sprinkle plenty of the seed mix on top for an easy, balanced and delicious breakfast.

Adaptations for the whole family: This is delicious as it is. You can easily turn it into a pudding by sprinkling oats and the seed mix on top of the fruit and serving it with some custard. Add a drizzle of honey, if you like, for older kids and adults.

Continued overleaf →

Tip: Use up any leftover plums in the Plum and Banana Teething Biscuit recipe on page 107 and use the pears in place of the avocado in my Avocado and Raspberry Muffins on page 96. You can use frozen pears/plums if easier.

Switching ingredients in/out: Swap the plums and pears for any other fruits.

Storing leftovers/how to defrost: The seed mix will keep in an airtight container in the fridge for 4–6 months. For the stewed fruit, cool it to room temperature within 2 hours. Place into an airtight container in the fridge and eat within 2 days. Alternatively, place in the freezer and consume within 3 months. Defrost in the fridge overnight or until fully thawed. Reheat until piping hot and then allow to cool before serving.

Baby Brekkie Biscuits

I had originally planned to make these a version of the biscuits you see in the breakfast aisle, but it turns out it's *very* hard to make that kind of biscuit without any added sugars. I made these ones on a whim and they're honestly delicious, with a slightly sweet taste and a crumbly texture!

Prep: 15 minutes
Cook: 12–15 minutes
Makes: 10–12 biscuits

125g porridge oats
80g unsalted butter, softened, or plant-based spread
1 tbsp ground flaxseed
1 tbsp milk of choice
1 tbsp Super Duper Seed Mix (see page 125, or any ground seeds/nuts will do)
3 tbsp apple sauce (with no added sugar)
1 tsp ground cinnamon

1 Preheat the oven to 220°C/200°C fan. Line a large baking sheet with greaseproof paper.

2 In a bowl, combine all the ingredients and mix until it forms a thick paste.

3 Take a tablespoon of the mix and roll it in your hands to form a ball. Pop it onto the lined tray and push down a little to create a round biscuit. Repeat with the rest of the mixture until you have 10–12 biscuits, placed about 5cm apart from each other.

4 Bake in the middle of the oven for 12–15 minutes, or until golden and crispy.

5 Leave to cool on the tray for 5 minutes, then remove to a cooling rack.

6 Serve as a brekkie on the go.

Serving ideas: Serve with a dollop of yoghurt to dip in and a sprinkle of Super Duper Seed Mix on top!

Adaptations for adults: This recipe works well with a handful of chocolate chips thrown into the mix for adults and older kids. Alternatively, add some extra apple sauce on the side as a dip. I love these just as they are though.

Storing leftovers/how to defrost: Will keep in an airtight container in the fridge for 2–3 days or in the freezer for 3–4 months. Thoroughly defrost in the fridge overnight.

Tip: Sometimes it can be hard to get apple sauce without a lot of added sugar, but it does exist. Health food stores do versions, but you can also just use a 100 per cent apple puree baby pouch, or make it yourself by boiling or steaming peeled apple pieces until soft and blending – I promise it's worth it for these biscuits!

Lunches

At our house, picky lunches are essential at the weekend – foods like sandwiches, crackers and oatcakes that you can easily carry out and about with lots of spreads and boxes of chopped veggie sticks, fruit and hummus make things as easy as pie. However, with these lunches, I wanted to offer something a bit different.

Some of these recipes are more experimental and take a little longer, while others are nice, quick lunches you can whip up in a few minutes. I've tried to pack in the nutrients and the flavours, while being a little experimental with the textures too. If you need to adapt the textures, you can easily give things a chop, mash or blend, or dissect the meals and offer your baby individual ingredients as finger foods.

I love meals that are versatile and can work as a picnic, a snack or be bulked out into a lunch or dinner, so there are a lot of these kinds of options here too. Enjoy!

Cheesy Parsnip Muffins

These muffins have such a fab flavour and are so moreish! I love a muffin, as you can probably tell, but I also love bakes and cakes where you can get some added extras in, like with these veggie muffins with parsnips and sweetcorn as well as milled seeds. There are lots of nutrients in these and they taste great. Cut the muffins into finger sticks if it's easier for younger babies. These are fab for lunch teamed up with some veggie sticks, a dip or a mini salad, and are great for packed lunches and on the go too!

Prep: 5 minutes
Cook: 20–25 minutes
Makes: 8 muffins

2 large free-range eggs or 2 flaxseed eggs (see page 40)
198g tin sweetcorn, drained
120g self-raising flour
1 tbsp mixed ground seeds or my Super Duper Seed Mix (see page 125, without dried fruit)
100g parsnips, peeled and coarsely grated
50g Cheddar cheese, coarsely grated

1   Preheat the oven to 200°C/180°C fan. Line a cupcake or muffin tin with 8 cases.

2   Add the eggs and sweetcorn to a food processor and whizz until combined. Add the flour and mixed ground seeds and mix in with a spoon. Then mix in the parsnips and half the cheese, again with a spoon (don't whizz it as you want to keep the texture).

3   Divide the mixture between the cases, then sprinkle over the remaining cheese. Bake in the middle of the oven for 20–25 minutes, or until golden and cooked through.

4   Leave to cool in the tray for about 5 minutes, then remove to a cooling rack.

Switching ingredients in/out: You can use other grated veggies like carrot or courgette, but it might change the texture when baked. You can swap the cheese for a dairy-free alternative (or leave it out) and you can leave out the milled seeds (add an extra 1 tablespoon of flour instead) if you prefer too.

Storing leftovers/how to defrost: Cool to room temperature within 2 hours. Place into an airtight container in the fridge and eat within 2 days. Alternatively, place in the freezer and consume within 3 months. Defrost in the fridge overnight or until fully thawed.

Tip: You can blend the eggs and sweetcorn with a hand blender if you prefer and then just stir through the flour, seeds, parsnips and cheese. Use up any leftover parsnips in the Veg Soup on page 138.

Quick Tomato Prawnzo

I absolutely love this fresh and delicious prawnzo! It's a winner in our house and is such a quick one to prep. It's also really versatile and it's easy to make it vegan by using tofu instead of prawns. Personally, I think the lemon makes it, but I'll let you decide. Finely chop the veggies and prawns for younger babies, or leave it chunkier if serving to toddlers and older kids.

Prep: 5 minutes
Cook: 15–20 minutes
Serves: 1 adult and 2 babies/toddlers, with leftovers

½ tbsp olive oil
2 garlic cloves, peeled and crushed
150g cherry tomatoes, quartered
150g orzo
180g frozen peeled prawns, finely chopped (avoid cutting prawns in rounds for little ones – slice lengthways before finely chopping) or 60g tofu
handful of green beans (about 60g), fresh or frozen, thinly sliced or chopped
juice of 1 lemon

1 Heat the oil in a medium lidded saucepan over a medium heat. Add the garlic and cook for a few minutes, then add the tomatoes and cook for 2 more minutes, stirring to combine.

2 Add the orzo, 350 millilitres of water and the prawns and give it a stir. Bring to the boil, then turn down to a simmer. Add the green beans, stirring to combine, then pop the lid on for 5 minutes.

3 Cook for a further 5 minutes without the lid on, stirring again. If using tofu, crumble in now and give it a stir to warm through.

4 Give the dish a squeeze of lemon before serving.

Storing leftovers/how to defrost: Cool to room temperature within 2 hours. Place into an airtight container in the fridge and eat within 2 days. Alternatively, place in the freezer and consume within 3 months. Defrost in the fridge overnight or until fully thawed. Reheat until piping hot and then allow to cool before serving.

Cauliflower 'Chicken' Nuggets and Chips

These little veggie takes on chicken nuggets are super delicious and packed with flavours which really come through with the cauliflower as a base. They are pretty easy to make and bring out for lunchtime and are definitely something all the family will enjoy. I've made them with chips here, but you can easily just have some nuggets on their own as a snack or make a bigger meal out of them too.

Prep: 15 minutes
Cook: 1 hour
Makes: 30–40 nuggets (serves 1 adult and 2 babies/toddlers, plus extras for freezing)

1 tbsp ground flaxseed
2 tbsp boiling water
500g Maris Piper potatoes, skin on, cut into long chips
1 medium cauliflower (about 650g), trimmed and cut into florets, stalks chopped up well
150g homemade or shop-bought breadcrumbs
60g Cheddar cheese, grated
1 tsp garlic powder

Tip: To make your own breadcrumbs, just whizz up 2 slices of good-quality bread (wholemeal if possible) in a blender or food processor.

1   Preheat the oven to 200°C/180°C fan. Line two large baking trays with greaseproof paper.

2   Bring a large saucepan of water to the boil.

3   In a small bowl, mix the flaxseed with 2 tbsp boiling water. Give it a mix, then leave to one side.

4   Put the potato chips onto one of the lined trays and cook for 35–40 minutes, checking them halfway through and moving them around so they do not catch and brown too much.

5   Once the water has come to the boil, add the cauliflower and cook for around 8 minutes (or until soft). Drain and leave to steam-dry for around 5 minutes. (It is really important to let it steam-dry to get rid of the excess water.)

6   Pop the cooked cauliflower back into the dry saucepan and mash well, then add the breadcrumbs, cheese, garlic powder and thickened flaxseed mix. Mix together until it is all combined. The mix should be able to be formed into nuggets, but also not be too dry.

7   Scrunch the mixture together to form around 30–40 nugget-shaped pieces (about 4.5cm wide). If the mix feels too wet to shape, add a few more breadcrumbs.

8   Pop them all onto the remaining lined tray and bake in the middle of the oven for 25–30 minutes, turning halfway, or until golden and crisp.

9   Serve the nuggets with some of the chips as finger foods.

Serving ideas: Serve with my red pepper dip (see page 80) and a side of steamed frozen and squashed peas.

Switching ingredients in/out: You can swap the flaxseed for a small chicken's egg, leave out the cheese or swap it for a non-dairy alternative or even use nutritional yeast, if preferred. You can also use gluten-free bread/breadcrumbs.

Adaptations for the whole family: Add a little spice to the cauliflower mix before shaping into nuggets.

Storing leftovers/how to defrost: These are best eaten straight out of the oven as they go a bit soggy when kept. If you are storing, cool to room temperature within 2 hours. Place into an airtight container in the fridge and eat within 2 days. Alternatively, place in the freezer and consume within 3 months. Defrost in the fridge overnight or until fully thawed. Reheat until piping hot and then allow to cool before serving.

Pinwheel Wraps

This is a unique take on a wrap – chopped up into mini pinwheels for little ones. I think this recipe is so fresh, fruity and delicious. It's a tricky one for *really* little babies to manage, but it's good for helping them to explore new textures. Allow them to dissect the wraps and eat them as they can, or squash them together really well so they have more of a chance of holding them.

Prep: 5 minutes
Cook: 20–25 minutes
Serves: 1 adult and 2 babies/toddlers

1 free-range skinless and boneless chicken breast (about 120g) or 60g tofu
1 tbsp olive oil
2 wheat and wholemeal large wraps
2 tbsp thick Greek yoghurt or non-dairy alternative
handful of spinach, washed and finely chopped
1 small apple, cored and grated
½ tbsp nutritional yeast

1 Preheat the oven to 200°C/180°C fan. Pop the chicken breast on a baking tray, drizzle with oil and bake for 20–25 minutes until the chicken is cooked through. Leave to one side and shred when cool enough to handle.

2 On a clean board, lay out the wraps, dollop each with yoghurt, then spread it evenly over the whole wrap surface.

3 Lay the shredded chicken down the middle of each of the wraps (or crumble in the tofu), then do the same with the chopped spinach and grated apple. Sprinkle over the nutritional yeast, then roll up each wrap really tightly.

4 Cut one wrap into 2-cm thick rounds and pop on a plate for your little one. You can just eat yours as a wrap or cut in half and enjoy.

Adaptations for the whole family: These have a lovely, fresh taste as they are, but you could add some hot sauce and more salad leaves.

Storing leftovers: Cool to room temperature within 2 hours. Place into an airtight container in the fridge and eat within 2 days.

Mini Mexican Burgers with Tomato Salsa

 Ve

These Mexican burger bites are such a simple little recipe. Make plenty so you can pop some in the freezer for another day. They are fab bulked out with a burger bun and some extra veg to make a full meal for your baby or toddler, but also work well as a little snack with a dip. There are lots of flavours and nutrients in this plant-based dish!

Prep: 10–15 minutes
Cook: 10–15 minutes
Makes: around 10 mini burgers

60g porridge oats
100g medium chestnut mushrooms (about 4–8), quartered
400g tin black beans, drained and rinsed
1 tsp ground cumin
1 tsp smoked paprika
1 tsp garlic powder
1 small carrot (about 30g), peeled and coarsely grated
½ tbsp olive oil, if frying

For the tomato salsa:
1 spring onion, trimmed and very finely chopped
150g ripe medium tomatoes, very finely chopped
a few sprigs of coriander, leaves picked and very finely chopped (optional)

1 If you are oven-cooking the burgers, preheat the oven to 200°C/180°C fan.

2 In a food processor, add the oats and blend up to a rough flour. Add the mushrooms and pulse again until it combines and forms a chunky mix.

3 Add in the black beans, spices and garlic powder. Pulse until the beans are broken down, but bits are still visible (though ensure there are no whole beans). Add in the grated carrot and mix well.

4 Remove to a clean surface and roll into around 10–12 golf-ball-sized balls, then flatten between your hands (about 3cm thick).

5 Pop the burgers onto the lined tray and cook in the oven for 10–15 minutes, turning halfway, until golden and crispy. Alternatively, heat the oil in a large frying pan over a medium heat. Add the burgers and cook for 3–4 minutes on each side until nice and crispy.

6 Meanwhile, to make the salsa, add the spring onions, tomatoes and coriander leaves (if using) to a bowl and give it a good mix.

7 Serve the mini burgers as a little bite for your baby with the salsa as a side dip.

Serving ideas: Top with yoghurt or sour cream and the tomato salsa and pop in a burger bun (two can easily fit in one bun).

Adaptations for the whole family: Add some mayo and some spicy salsa and a squeeze of lime when serving yours, if you prefer.

Storing leftovers/how to defrost: Cool to room temperature within 2 hours. Place into an airtight container in the fridge and eat within 2 days. Alternatively, place the burgers in the freezer with baking paper between and consume within 3 months. Defrost in the fridge overnight or until fully thawed. Reheat until piping hot and then allow to cool before serving.

Tip: You can use any leftover chestnut mushrooms in the Creamy Mushroom Toast Topping recipe on page 69.

Veg Soup with Garlic Batons

Sometimes soups can be really hit and miss with little ones, but I love soups as an easy way to get *lots* of veggies in in one go and also as a fab way to use up any leftovers. Soup is also a lovely, warming meal and, to this day, it's always what I crave when I'm unwell. This recipe is a nutrient-packed and flavourful soup that your little ones will love. Try serving it to them with the garlic batons to dip in so they can do some self-feeding. You can also vary the texture when you blend it and make it a bit thicker for older children and thinner for little ones – whatever works for you and your family! Go easy on the garlic on the batons for younger babies who haven't had a lot of garlic before.

Prep: 15 minutes
Cook: 30–35 minutes
Serves: 1 adult and 2 babies/toddlers, with leftovers for another day

250g white bread, cut into batons
1½ tbsp olive oil
1–2 medium garlic cloves, peeled and crushed
1 white onion, peeled and roughly chopped
1 stick of celery, trimmed and roughly chopped
1 sprig of rosemary, leaves picked and finely chopped or 1 tbsp dried rosemary
1–2 medium parsnips (about 300g), peeled and roughly chopped
300g butternut squash, peeled and seeds removed, cut into 2cm chunks or sweet potato, peeled and cut into 2cm chunks
1 medium potato (about 200g), peeled and roughly chopped
½ x 400g tin chickpeas, butter beans or cannellini, drained and rinsed (optional)

1　Pop the bread batons onto a baking tray.

2　In a small bowl, mix 1 tablespoon of the oil with the crushed garlic. Spread the mix over the top of the bread batons.

3　Heat the remaining oil in a large non-stick pan over a medium heat.

4　Add the onion, celery and rosemary and cook for 10–15 minutes, stirring occasionally.

5　Preheat the oven to 200°C/180°C fan.

6　Once the onion and celery have softened, add the parsnips, butternut squash or sweet potato and the potato. Add 1 litre of water and bring to the boil. Cook for 15 minutes with the lid on, or until the potato is cooked. Add the chickpeas/beans (if using) and warm through for a couple of minutes.

7　Meanwhile, bake the bread in the oven for 10–15 minutes, or until golden and crisp.

8　Blend the soup to your desired consistency – chunky, thick or thin – and serve with the garlic batons. Chop the batons into thin sticks for your baby to munch on, cutting off any really hard edges.

Storing leftovers/how to defrost: Cool to room temperature within 2 hours. Place into an airtight container in the fridge and eat within 2 days. Alternatively, portion into batches, place in the freezer and consume within 3 months. Defrost in the fridge overnight or until fully thawed. Reheat until piping hot and then allow to cool before serving.

Microwave Risotto

I wanted to include this microwave dish in this book as a *super* quick version of a risotto for families. If you prefer, you can cook this in the oven too. Just preheat the oven to 200°C/180°C fan, add all the ingredients to a shallow casserole pan, pop a lid on and place it in the oven for 30 minutes – the results are the same.
I love the extra flavours and colours in this as, sometimes, risottos can look a little boring. It's a regular go-to now in our house as it's so speedy and nutrient-rich. You can make this one with water instead of the low-salt stock, if you prefer, but it will need some added flavours for adults!

Prep: 5 minutes
Cook: 15 minutes
Serves: 1 adult and
2 babies/toddlers

200g risotto rice
2 spring onions, trimmed and
　finely chopped
2 garlic cloves, peeled and
　crushed
1 carrot, peeled and finely
　grated
1 tsp dried herbs (coriander,
　thyme and basil work well)
630ml low-/no salt stock
3 tbsp nutritional yeast
　(optional)
120g tinned cannellini or borlotti
　beans, drained and rinsed
　(mashed for babies)

1　In a large microwavable bowl, add the rice, spring onions, garlic, carrot and dried herbs. Give it a good mix then pour over 430ml of the stock and cover with a plate or cling film. Microwave on high setting for 10 minutes.

2　Carefully remove the plate or pull back the cling film and stir the mix (it should be nearly cooked by now and the liquid absorbed). Add the remaining stock, nutritional yeast (if using) and beans, give it another mix and put the plate/cling film back on top. Cook for another 5 minutes.

3　Leave to stand for 5 minutes and check the rice is cooked. (As microwaves vary, don't worry if it isn't – just pop it back in for a few more minutes until the rice is cooked, adding an extra splash of stock or water if it is drying out too much.)

4　Give the risotto a little mash before serving to younger babies and offer on a spoon. You can also roll it into rice balls when it's fully cool and serve to your baby as finger food.

Adaptations for the whole family: Season your portion and add Parmesan and a little butter while the risotto is resting.

Storing leftovers/how to defrost: Cool to room temperature within 1 hour. Place into an airtight container in the fridge and eat within 24 hours. Alternatively, portion into batches, place in the freezer and consume within 1 month. Defrost in the fridge overnight or until fully thawed. Reheat until steaming hot all the way through, mixing halfway, and then allow to cool before serving. Do not reheat rice more than once.

Monster Pancakes: Take Two

In *How to Feed Your Toddler*, I created a very popular Spinach Monster Pancakes recipe that's super green. I wanted to do another one for this book that's super purple, and so pleasing visually for little ones. This is kind of a mix between a pancake and an omelette – it looks fab and should brighten any baby/toddler's plate. You might want to add some cheese or nutritional yeast to your pancake as it doesn't have any extra spices in, but it's perfect for babies and toddlers as it is.

Prep: 5 minutes
Cook: 10–12 minutes
Serves: 1 adult and 2 babies/toddlers

100g vacuum-packed beetroot in natural juices, drained
1 large free-range egg or 1 flaxseed egg (see page 40)
60ml milk of choice
110g self-raising flour
15g nutritional yeast or 30g Cheddar cheese, grated (optional)
35g red pepper, deseeded and thinly chopped or cut into thin strips
handful of frozen peas, mashed for younger babies
drizzle of olive oil

1 Add the beetroot, egg and milk to a blender. Blitz to make a purple batter.

2 In a large bowl, add the flour, then pour in the batter and whisk to combine. Sprinkle in the nutritional yeast or cheese (if using) and add the red pepper and peas, giving it a mix. Leave to one side.

3 Preheat the grill to the highest temperature.

4 Heat the oil in a small ovenproof non-stick frying pan over a medium heat. Once the pan is hot, pour in the batter and spread out to cover the whole pan. Cook for 3–4 minutes, then put under the grill for 6–8 minutes until puffed up and cooked through.

5 Leave to cool a little, then slice into wedges or fingers for your little one to munch on.

Serving ideas: Serve with some fresh chopped tomatoes or hummus as a dip.

Adaptations for the whole family: For your portion, slice in some red chilli or sprinkle some feta on top of the pancakes before they go under the grill.

Storing leftovers/how to defrost: Cool to room temperature within 2 hours. Place into an airtight container in the fridge and eat within 2 days. Alternatively, place in the freezer and consume within 3 months. Defrost in the fridge overnight or until fully thawed. Reheat until piping hot and then allow to cool before serving.

Fruity Tofu Fried Rice

Tofu fried rice is a dish I've been making for my family for years and it's one of Raffy's all-time favourite meals – but this one has a fruity twist. Although they might seem strange additions at first, the pineapple and orange really add a fresh and delicious kick. This is a simple one-panner so is an easy lunch to prepare and you can always swap the tofu for eggs if you prefer.

Prep: 5 minutes
Cook: 15 minutes
Serves: 2 adults and
2 babies/toddlers

2 tbsp sesame oil
2 tbsp smooth peanut butter
juice of 1 large orange
a few rings of tinned pineapple (in natural juices), drained and finely chopped
1 garlic clove, peeled and crushed
2 spring onions, trimmed and thinly sliced
150g firm tofu, crumbled
250g pouch of cooked basmati rice
120g peas, mashed slightly, or green beans, finely chopped

1 In a small bowl, mix together 1 tablespoon of the sesame oil, the peanut butter, half the orange juice and the pineapple pieces. You may need to mix this really well to remove any peanut butter lumps. Leave to one side for later.

2 Heat the remaining sesame oil in a wok or medium frying pan over a medium heat. Add the garlic, spring onions and crumbled tofu. Cook for about 5 minutes, breaking up the tofu more until it starts to get crispy.

3 Add the rice and the other half of the orange juice and the peas or green beans, and cook for 10 minutes, stirring occasionally, until the rice is piping hot and the veggies are cooked and soft.

4 Take the pan off the heat, drizzle over the peanut sauce and give it a good mix before serving. If you fancy, offer a whole pineapple ring on the side for your baby/toddler to explore.

Adaptations for the whole family: Serve with some sweet chilli sauce or a chopped fresh chilli on top if you fancy it.

Storing leftovers/how to defrost: To be eaten fresh – do not store or reheat.

Easy Ratatouille

Ratatouille is a recipe I grew up having as a child, but I was not always the biggest fan of it. These days, though, it's one of my favourite ways to make a simple, veg-packed and tasty one-panner. Prep this ahead and just pop it all in a tray in the oven the night before, then leave it to cook away when you're ready. This is a really versatile recipe and is a good way of exploring some of those Mediterranean veggies with your little one. Dice the veggies smaller for younger babies and offer it on a spoon, or leave the veggies chunkier for older kids to explore a bit more texture. The veggies all go super soft anyway. Top with cheese or serve with bread and hummus – whatever you fancy!

Prep: 15 minutes
Cook: 25–55 minutes
Serves: 1 adult and 2 babies/toddlers, with leftovers for another day

½ coloured pepper, deseeded and finely chopped
1 small red onion, peeled and finely chopped
100g aubergine, finely diced
1 garlic clove, peeled and finely chopped
100g fresh cherry tomatoes, quartered
1 tbsp olive oil
½ tbsp dried oregano
400g tin chopped tomatoes

1 Preheat the oven to 200°C/180°C fan.

2 Pop all the veggies, garlic and cherry tomatoes into a roasting tray and drizzle with the oil. Sprinkle over the dried oregano and give it a good mix.

3 Cook in the middle of the oven for 25 minutes.

4 Carefully remove the tray and add the tinned tomatoes and a good splash of water. Cook for another 20–30 minutes (depending on how big you have chopped your veggies; if you have cut them small it won't need all this extra time).

5 Allow to cool a little before serving to your baby in a bowl with a spoon. Blend or mash for your baby as you see fit, or serve as it is.

Serving ideas: Serve alongside rice or couscous.

Adaptations for the whole family: Leave the veggies a bit chunkier on one side of the tin if you prefer a chunky ratatouille. I actually quite like it chopped small with some delicious bread for dipping in it.

Storing leftovers/how to defrost: Cool to room temperature within 2 hours. Place into an airtight container in the fridge and eat within 2 days. Alternatively, place in the freezer and consume within 3 months. Defrost in the fridge overnight or until fully thawed. Reheat until piping hot and then allow to cool before serving.

Rainbow Mac and Cheese

Our family *loves* a mac and cheese, and you'll probably notice that from the amount of mac and cheese recipes I have! But each one of them is different as I feel like you can do so much with this dish. This is a rainbow one, as it adds lots of colour and is packed with veggies. It works really well as a simple family favourite – so tasty!

Prep: 10 minutes
Cook: 30–35 minutes
Serves: 1 adult and 2 babies/toddlers, with leftovers

80g frozen (or fresh) green beans
1 tbsp unsalted butter, dairy-free spread or olive oil, plus an extra splash of oil
½ white onion, peeled and finely chopped
1 carrot, peeled and finely grated
½ coloured pepper, deseeded and finely chopped
1 tbsp plain flour
350ml milk of choice
200g pasta shapes
100g broccoli, trimmed and stalk and florets roughly chopped
30g mature Cheddar cheese, grated
1 tbsp ground almonds (optional)

Adaptations for the whole family: Season and serve with a hearty rocket salad and add some extra cheese to your portion if you prefer.

1 Get the green beans out of the freezer if using frozen.

2 Heat the splash of oil in a casserole type pan over a medium heat. Add the onion, carrot and pepper and cook for 10 minutes until softened, then stir in the flour, then the milk, slowly mixing each time to create a thick sauce. Simmer over a low heat for around 8 minutes, stirring frequently so it doesn't get lumpy or catch. Once thickened, remove from the heat.

3 While the sauce is cooking, cook the pasta according to the packet instructions, popping a sieve or colander on top of the pasta pan and steaming the green beans and broccoli for 5 minutes (or until cooked through). Once the pasta and veg are cooked, remove the colander and drain the pasta, reserving a good splash of the starchy pasta water in a mug to one side. Decant the pasta into an ovenproof dish (about 18 x 25cm).

4 Preheat the oven to 200°C/180°C fan.

5 Add the green beans and broccoli to a blender along with half of the creamy carrot sauce and the pasta water and whizz up to create a lovely green sauce.

6 Stir the blended sauce through the cooked pasta (along with the leftover unblended base mix). Sprinkle over the grated cheese and ground almonds (if using), then bake in the middle of the oven for 15 minutes until golden and looking delicious.

Switching ingredients in/out: If you want to make this dairy-free, just leave out the cheese and add more almonds.

Storing leftovers/how to defrost: Cool to room temperature within 2 hours. Place into an airtight container in the fridge and eat within 2 days. Alternatively, place in the freezer and consume within 3 months. Defrost in the fridge overnight or until fully thawed. Reheat until piping hot and then allow to cool before serving.

Butternut Squash Dhal

This naturally creamy dhal is super easy to pop in a pan and leave to cook. Everyone in our family loves this recipe and it's such a nutrient-dense option too. Because it's cooked for 40 minutes, the veggies are super soft and easy to mash down a little for younger babies or leave chunky for older kids. It's really flavourful, but without the heat, which you can start experimenting with as your baby gets more familiar with spices. As with a couple of the recipes in previous sections, it can be tricky to find no added salt curry powder. It's OK if you only have curry powder with salt in it – just be mindful of how much you use in your baby's portion.

Prep: 10 minutes
Cook: 35–45 minutes
Serves: 1 adult and 2 babies/toddlers, with leftovers for another day

drizzle of olive oil
½ tsp ground turmeric
½ tsp no added salt mild curry powder
½ white onion, peeled and finely chopped
1 garlic clove, peeled and finely chopped
1cm piece of fresh ginger, peeled and finely chopped or ½ tsp ground ginger
300g butternut squash, peeled and seeds removed, cut into 2cm chunks, or sweet potato, peeled and cut into 2cm chunks
1 tbsp tomato puree
200g dried red lentils, rinsed

1 Heat the oil in a lidded heavy-based saucepan over a medium heat. Add the turmeric and curry powder along with the onion, garlic and ginger and cook for 5 minutes, stirring occasionally.

2 Add the butternut squash (or sweet potato), tomato puree, lentils and 800 millilitres of water. Bring to the boil, then turn down to a simmer, pop the lid on and cook for 30–40 minutes (or until thickened and the lentils are cooked). Be sure to check the pan halfway and give it a stir. Remove the lid and leave it off for the last 5 minutes or so.

3 Once cooked, serve to your baby with a spoon.

Serving ideas: This is delicious served with toasted pitta fingers, natural or dairy-free yoghurt and some nigella/black onions seeds sprinkled on top.

Adaptations for the whole family: Cut the veg so it is chunkier or tear in some spinach leaves.

Storing leftover/how to defrost: Cool to room temperature within 2 hours. Place into an airtight container in the fridge and eat within 2 days. Alternatively, place in the freezer and consume within 3 months. Defrost in the fridge overnight or until fully thawed. Reheat until piping hot and then allow to cool before serving.

Easy Chicken Satay

This is a really simple but tasty recipe, with a bit of novelty for the older kids too as it's served on kebab sticks! This is a great one to get older children involved in making with you as well. I absolutely love the flavour combinations in this and I've made it very successfully with tofu too. It's delicious and makes a light lunch, though you can always bulk it out with other leftovers on the side.

Prep: 10 minutes
Cook: 15 minutes
Makes: 4 skewers (serves 1 adult and 1 baby/toddler)

2 free-range skinless and boneless chicken breasts (about 400g)
4 tbsp tinned coconut milk (shake the tin really well before measuring out)
2 tbsp smooth peanut butter
juice of ½ lime
1 tsp sesame oil
1 garlic clove, peeled and crushed
a few tsp of sesame seeds (optional)

Serving ideas: Serve with some toasted pitta sticks, crunchy salad leaves and finely shredded sugar snap peas.

Tip: Add more lime for more of a zing and serve with minty yoghurt as an added dip. Use up the leftover coconut milk in the Mango and Coconut Ice Cream recipe on page 211.

1   Preheat the oven to 200°C/180°C fan. Line a baking tray with greaseproof paper.

2   Place the chicken breasts between two pieces of greaseproof paper and gently bash them with a rolling pin (or the bottom of a frying pan) until they are about 1cm thick. Remove the paper and discard.

3   Cut the chicken into strips and thread them evenly onto 4 skewers. Pop the skewers onto the lined tray and cook for 10 minutes, turning halfway through.

4   In a small bowl, mix together the coconut milk, peanut butter, lime juice and 1 tablespoon of water until there are no lumps.

5   Meanwhile, heat the sesame oil in a frying pan over a medium heat. Add the garlic and cook for 1 minute, then pour in the peanut mix, stirring it to allow it to thicken a bit (this will only take a minute).

6   Remove half of the peanut mix from the pan and add it to a bowl for serving later on.

7   Remove the chicken skewers from the oven and brush with the remaining sauce mix, making sure it covers all the chicken pieces. Sprinkle over the sesame seeds (if using) and return to the oven for 5 more minutes, or until juices run clear and the chicken is cooked though.

8   Remove the skewers from the oven, sliding the chicken off the skewers onto a plate for babies and toddlers. Serve with the reserved peanut sauce for dipping.

Storing leftovers/how to defrost: Cool to room temperature within 2 hours. Place into an airtight container in the fridge and eat within 2 days. Alternatively, place in the freezer and consume within 3 months. Defrost in the fridge overnight or until fully thawed. Reheat until piping hot and then allow to cool before serving.

Tomato Soup

This is my take on a very popular tomato soup that the kids and I have when we're not feeling too well. I love a straight-up tomato soup like this – it's nice and smooth and is perfect for dipping bread into. This one is quick, easy and delicious, but without the salt and sugar you find in the shop-bought ones.

Prep: 5 minutes
Cook: 10–12 minutes
Serves: 1 adult and 2 babies/toddlers, with leftovers

1 tbsp olive oil
½ white onion, peeled and roughly chopped
1–2 garlic cloves, peeled and crushed
1 stick of celery, chopped
a few sprigs of thyme, leaves picked
200g ripe cherry tomatoes, halved
250ml no added sugar passata
150g tinned butter beans, drained and rinsed

1 Heat the oil in a large saucepan over a medium heat. Add the onion, garlic, celery and thyme leaves. Cook for 5 minutes, stirring occasionally.

2 Stir in the tomatoes and cook for a further 5 minutes.

3 Pour in the passata and 250 millilitres of water. Bring to the boil, then turn off the heat.

4 Add in the butter beans and blend it all as smoothly as you can before serving.

Serving ideas: Serve with a dollop of yoghurt or plant-based alternative and sprinkle with some of my Super Duper Seed Mix (see page 125).

Adaptations for the whole family: You could sprinkle some chilli flakes or toasted seeds on top of your portion. Season with salt and pepper, if preferred.

Storing leftovers/how to defrost: Cool to room temperature within 2 hours. Place into an airtight container in the fridge and eat within 2 days. Alternatively, portion into batches, place in the freezer and consume within 3 months. Defrost in the fridge overnight or until fully thawed. Reheat until piping hot and then allow to cool before serving.

Mini Broccoli Dauphinoise Squares

I love the idea of these little potato squares that add veggies and plenty of flavour and can be eaten for lunch on the go, as a snack or bulked out with extra veggies and some protein as a larger meal. Feel free to swap out the broccoli for other veg, but these are really easy wins and are super simple to put together. Serve them as squares or offer them as thin finger foods for younger babies to self-feed. I hope you enjoy these – they are delicious!

Prep: 10 minutes
Cook: 25–30 minutes
Makes: 8 squares

340g (about 2 medium) potatoes, skin on
100g broccoli, finely chopped
120g self-raising flour
2 large free-range eggs
good pinch of oregano
1 tsp garlic powder or chopped chives
70g Parmesan, Cheddar or grated mozzarella cheese

1 Preheat the oven to 200°C/180°C fan. Line a 20 x 20cm ovenproof dish or loaf tin with greaseproof paper.

2 Grate the potatoes into a bowl and squeeze them really well to get out the excess liquid. Put the squeezed potato into another large bowl, discarding the liquid.

3 Add the broccoli, flour, eggs, oregano, garlic powder and most of the cheese to the potato. Give it a good mix.

4 Tip the mixture into the prepared dish and spread it out to around 2–2.5cm thick, roughly smoothing the top. Sprinkle on the remaining cheese and bake in the middle of the oven for 25–30 minutes, or until golden and set.

5 Leave to cool a little before cutting into around 8 equal squares or 16 fingers, depending on your baby/toddler's age.

Serving ideas: Serve with a little side salad (try the Megamix Pasta Salad on page 178 or Baby's First 'Salad' on page 191).

Storing leftovers/how to defrost: Cool to room temperature within 2 hours. Place into an airtight container in the fridge and eat within 2 days. Alternatively, place in the freezer and consume within 3 months. Defrost in the fridge overnight or until fully thawed. Reheat until piping hot and then allow to cool before serving.

Avo, Broccoli and Peanut Butter Toast Topping

This quirky little toast topping is something you'd normally find in one of those delicious 'cheffy' cookbooks, but I've tweaked it for little ones and added plenty of flavours and nutrients. This recipe is perfect if you have a broccoli floret or two leftover that needs using up and, if you like peanut butter, you won't regret trying it – this one is so delicious. It's become a new favourite toast topping in our house.

Prep: 5 minutes
Cook: 5–6 minutes
Serves: 1 adult and 2 babies/ toddlers

30g broccoli, cut into small pieces, stalks removed, or 50g leftover cooked broccoli
50g ripe avocado, mashed
1 tbsp good-quality smooth peanut butter
a squeeze of lemon
3 slices of good-quality bread (wholemeal if possible)

1 In a small microwave bowl, add the broccoli and a good splash of water (about 2 tablespoons), cover with a plate or cling film and cook for 5 minutes on high. Alternatively, boil the broccoli for around 6 minutes.

2 Once the broccoli is cooked, drain and mash really well (or blend if your baby needs it). Add the avocado, mash them together to combine, and then stir in the peanut butter and lemon juice.

3 Toast the bread and spread the topping over the toast, then cut into fingers/triangles for your baby to self-feed (or whatever shape your baby/toddler likes!).

Adaptations for the whole family: You could have this with a poached egg on top with some salad and seeds. Or just drizzle some honey over the top!

Storing leftovers: This needs to be eaten fresh.

Tuna, Cheese and Sweet Potato Quesadilla

I love a quesadilla for babies as it's such a fab way to help them experiment with flavours and explore textures. Depending on your baby's age and stage, you might need to slice these up a little more or let your little one dissect them a bit and figure out how to eat them in their own way. I usually slice them up into wedges like a pizza for my two, but see what works best in your house. Adjust the amount of lemon zest you use depending on your baby's experience with lemon. You can vary the ingredients in these too – try meat, different fish, use different veggies, and so on. It's a fab and tasty option for a nice quick lunch!

Prep: 5–10 minutes
Cook: 12–18 minutes
Serves: 1 adult and 2 babies/toddlers

160g tin tuna (in spring water), drained
60g mature Cheddar cheese, grated
zest of ½–1 lemon
60g tinned pinto beans or chickpeas, drained, rinsed and roughly mashed
85g sweet potato, peeled and coarsely grated
4 large wholemeal wraps
2 heaped tbsp thick yoghurt or dairy-free alternative (optional)

1   In a bowl, mix together the tuna, cheese, lemon zest, beans or chickpeas and sweet potato, then leave to one side.

2   Heat a large non-stick frying pan over a medium heat, then add one of the wraps. Scatter the tuna mix evenly over the wrap, pop another wrap on top and press down to squash the filling together and seal.

3   Cook for 3–5 minutes, pressing it down well, then carefully flip/ turn to the other side and cook for a further 3 minutes until golden and crispy and the cheese has melted.

4   Remove to a board and repeat with the two remaining wraps.

5   Cut into wedges and serve with the yoghurt, if using, for dipping.

Serving ideas: Serve with a few cucumber sticks on the side.

Adaptations for the whole family: You could switch the tuna for tinned mackerel fillets and also add more cheese to your portion, if you prefer.

Storing leftovers: Best eaten fresh. Do not store or reheat.

Sushi Sandwiches

These little sushi roll-ups are a really lovely and exciting take on your sandwich filling. For younger babies who aren't used to finger foods and varied textures yet, these might be a little advanced. Older babies will be able to deconstruct the rolls and eat the matchstick-thin veggie sticks and the bread, but this recipe is probably more suitable for children over one, just because of the complexity and the mixed textures included in the ingredients. These look so fab and would be great on a party food platter or served as little picnic snacks. Use different things to spread on top for extra variety.

Prep: 10 minutes
Makes: 12 sushi pieces (serves 1 adult and 2 babies/toddlers)

3 slices of good-quality sliced bread (wholemeal if possible)
3–4 tbsp smooth peanut butter (or cream cheese or hummus)
30g red pepper, deseeded and sliced into matchsticks
30g cucumber, halved and sliced into matchsticks
1 chestnut mushroom, halved and thinly sliced
30g firm tofu, thinly sliced

1   Squash and flatten the slices of bread with a rolling pin. Trim the crusts off the bread (if they are very thick).

2   Spread the flattened bread slices with the peanut butter (or cream cheese or hummus), then pop the matchsticks of red pepper and cucumber, the sliced mushrooms and the tofu at the bottom of each slice of bread.

3   Roll up the bread slices, squashing the ends to seal it all up. Cut each into four equal pieces and then pop on a plate to serve, cut sides up so you can see the filling like sushi rolls.

Adaptations for the whole family: Dip the sushi sandwiches in soy or sweet chilli sauce to give your portion a bit of a kick.

Storing leftovers: Place into an airtight container in the fridge and eat within 2 days.

Image overleaf →

Carrot and Cauliflower Pasta

This is a super simple pasta dish that I just love. Because of the cauliflower, the sauce comes out really creamy and, of course, you can just vary the veggies that you use in it! There are so many ways to change it up and add toppings – and, if you're looking for extra protein, some red lentils or strips of chicken would work well too.

Prep: 5 minutes
Cook: 10 minutes (pasta depending)
Serves: 1 adult and 2 babies/ toddlers, with leftovers

200g pasta shapes
150g carrot, peeled and roughly chopped
150g cauliflower, trimmed and cut into chunks
50ml milk of choice
1 sprig of fresh thyme, leaves picked or ½ tbsp dried thyme
1–2 tbsp ground almonds (optional)

1 Cook the pasta according to the packet instructions. Pop a sieve or colander on top of the pasta pan and steam the cauliflower and carrot for 10 minutes (or until cooked through). Once cooked, remove the colander and drain the pasta, reserving 50 millilitres of the starchy pasta water.

2 Add the cauliflower, carrot and the reserved pasta water to a blender, along with the milk and thyme leaves. Blend until it creates a thick, creamy sauce.

3 Mix the sauce through the pasta and serve with a sprinkle of ground almonds if you fancy.

Adaptations for the whole family: Add a pinch of nutmeg or garlic powder along with the ground almonds. Or sprinkle some Parmesan on top. This also makes a sweet, fresh toast topping!

Storing leftovers/how to defrost: Cool to room temperature within 2 hours. Place into an airtight container in the fridge and eat within 2 days. Alternatively, place in the freezer and consume within 3 months. Defrost in the fridge overnight or until fully thawed. Reheat until piping hot and then allow to cool before serving.

Mini Pizza Pies

I love an easy cheesy potato pie and this is a fab take on that recipe (from my blog). This one adds a splash of colour and also some extra pizza-like flavours, making it really taste like pizza. This has always been a favourite recipe in our house and I love these new tweaks. If you want to add some iron-/protein-rich foods, you could serve it with an egg, mash in an egg with the potato or add some salmon on the side.

Prep: 10 minutes
Cook: 25–30 minutes
Serves: 1 adult and
1 baby/toddler

1 large potato (about 250g), peeled and cut into even chunks
50g frozen peas or other frozen veg such as green beans, chopped
1 spring onion, trimmed and finely chopped
35g cheese, grated, or 1 tbsp nutritional yeast
2 sprigs of fresh basil, leaves torn and roughly chopped (finely chopped for babies) or good pinch of dried oregano
1 tbsp tomato puree

1 Bring a large saucepan of water to the boil. Pop the potato pieces in and cook for 10–12 minutes until soft and you can put a knife through them easily. Add the frozen peas or other veg for the last 5 minutes.

2 Preheat the oven to 200°C/180°C fan.

3 Drain the potatoes and peas/veg and let them steam-dry for a few minutes, then mash them together really well. Add in the spring onion, half the cheese or all the nutritional yeast and the basil, then stir through the tomato puree.

4 Add the mix to two ramekins (8–10cm wide) or a single ovenproof dish, and sprinkle the remaining cheese on top.

5 Bake in the oven for 16–18 minutes, or until the top is golden and bubbling. Leave to cool or decant into a bowl before serving to your baby.

Serving ideas: Serve with beans or a side of broccoli.

Adaptations for the whole family: These pizza pies are delicious as they are, though you could add a few extra basil leaves or a little seasoning, as required, to your portion.

Storing leftovers/how to defrost: Cool to room temperature within 2 hours. Place into an airtight container in the fridge and eat within 2 days. Alternatively, place uncooked pies in the freezer and consume within 3 months. Defrost in the fridge overnight or until fully thawed and cook as per step 5 in the recipe instructions.

Tip: I often make this dish in bulk, freeze it and pop it out for an emergency meal.

Dinners

These recipes will help your baby/toddler continue to explore a variety of foods, moving them on to more 'family-style' meals that everyone can enjoy together. I've been a bit experimental with the textures used here, as, hopefully, your little one will have had plenty of experience with finger foods and self-feeding, and dabbled with the mashes and bridge meals on pages 57–71 too. However, it's super easy to blend, mash or chop where needed at any point. If you're unsure, I've given plenty of ideas on how to serve to babies throughout this section, but you know your own baby/toddler, so let them dictate what textures they need.

I've opted for a lot of plant-based options in this section and used plenty of beans, pulses and lentils as this is what I usually use when cooking at home, but if these are less familiar to you, check out the Alternatives Table on page 40 as it's so easy to swap other ingredients in.

Dinner is such an important meal for my family, but it's also often the hardest one to get 'right' at the end of the day, when tolerance is often minimal and you have tired little ones who just want their bed. The recipes are largely for 2 adults and 2 little ones, meaning that you may have plenty of leftovers to save you a day's cooking later down the line. The freezer is always your friend when it comes to evening meals!

I've used some of the recipes that I've found were super popular in my previous books and added twists and tweaks to make them exciting and new, like my Simple Cod Traybake (see page 186) and Mini Savoury Crumbles (see page 169) – one of my faves! I hope you enjoy sharing these recipes with your whole family.

Rainbow Baked Risotto

This is a super tasty dish with lots of added extra veggies – just how I like it! It looks fab and is an easy dinner option – it's just a case of chopping all the veggies and popping them into a big dish to cook in the oven; no more standing over the hob and stirring your risotto! You can add some protein by adding a tin of beans or lentils if you prefer or serve it with some chicken. I make it with water, but you could use stock if you prefer (ideally low-salt for babies). Babies should be able to easily eat this – just give it a little mash when it comes out, if needed, and make sure you chop all the veggies really finely at the start.

Prep: 10 minutes
Cook: 35 minutes
Serves: 2 adults and 2 babies/toddlers, with leftovers

1 white onion, peeled and finely chopped
1 garlic clove, peeled and crushed
250g risotto rice
1 medium parsnip (about 120g), peeled and coarsely grated
1 carrot, peeled and coarsely grated
1 small fresh beetroot (about 50g), washed and coarsely grated
30g asparagus or broccoli, finely chopped
30g Parmesan, grated, or 3 tbsp nutritional yeast
1 tbsp unsalted butter or dairy-free spread

1 Preheat the oven to 200°C/180°C fan.

2 Add 800 millilitres of water to a large lidded ovenproof casserole pan and bring to the boil.

3 Add all the ingredients (apart from the Parmesan/nutritional yeast and butter/spread) and give it a good stir. Cover with a lid and pop it into the oven for 35 minutes.

4 Once cooked, remove from the oven and stir in the Parmesan or nutritional yeast and the butter or spread, then give it a good stir.

Adaptations for the whole family: This may need a little seasoning if you're using water and not stock. Otherwise, it works perfectly as it is. Sprinkle some extra herbs or cheese on top, if needed!

Storing leftovers/how to defrost: Cool to room temperature within 1 hour. Place into an airtight container in the fridge and eat within 24 hours. Alternatively, portion into batches, place in the freezer and consume within 1 month. Defrost in the fridge overnight or until fully thawed. Reheat until steaming hot all the way through, mixing halfway, and then allow to cool before serving. Do not reheat rice more than once.

Baked Salmon Burrito

This is a fab and quirky little recipe, as well as an easy one. I made it for the family and also for my in-laws, and everyone loved it. It's got lots of flavour, colour, textures and nutrients, so is such a winner. Be a little careful as it comes out super hot and the textures might be tricky for younger babies. However, it should be a hit for toddlers – chop it into strips and flatten them a bit or let your little one dissect it and eat it as they like.

Prep: 5 minutes
Cook: 15 minutes
Serves: 1–2 adults and 2 babies/toddlers (4 burritos)

2 sustainable skinless and boneless salmon fillets (about 240g), cut into 1cm chunks
½ x 400g tin black beans, drained and rinsed
handful of ripe medium tomatoes (about 45g), sliced
45g spinach leaves, washed and very finely chopped
1 tsp smoked paprika
4–5 mini wholemeal wraps
50g Cheddar cheese, grated

1   Preheat the oven to 200°C/180°C fan.

2   In a bowl, mix the salmon, black beans, tomatoes, spinach and smoked paprika. Give it a good mix, mashing the beans a bit.

3   Place the wraps on a clean surface and divide the mixture between them. Sprinkle the cheese over each wrap. Tuck in the ends of the wrap, fold in the sides and fold in the top to enclose the filling. Continue until all the wraps are sealed.

4   Place on a lined baking tray sealed side down. Poke a few holes in the top of each before baking in the oven for 15 minutes until golden and the salmon is cooked through.

5   Serve the burritos whole for adults or allow to cool and cut in half for toddlers (a bit like a sandwich). For babies, cut the burritos into strips and give them a bit of a squash to flatten them before serving.

Serving ideas: Serve with the Cauliflower 'Chicken' Nuggets (see page 134) and a side salad.

Adaptations for the whole family: These are delicious as they are, but you might want to add some sweet chilli sauce or some chilli flakes to your parcel before wrapping.

Storing leftovers/how to defrost: Cool to room temperature within 1 hour. Wrap each in tinfoil and place into an airtight container in the fridge. Eat within 2 days. Alternatively, place in the freezer and consume within 1 month. Defrost in the fridge overnight or until fully thawed. Reheat within the foil in the oven until piping hot and then allow to cool before serving.

Mini Savoury Crumbles

I did a recipe similar to this in *How to Feed Your Family* and it was one of my favourites, so I wanted to recreate a version in this one too! This is so flavourful and really creamy, and the topping is perfect too. You could add some ground almonds to the topping or use wholemeal flour to add some extra nutrients. Give the kidney beans a mash before adding them into the mix if serving to little ones or blend a portion of the mix, pop it in a ramekin and add the topping before cooking it in the oven.

Prep: 15 minutes
Cook: 45–50 minutes
Serves: 2 adults and 2 babies/toddlers, with leftovers

2 large sweet potatoes (about 500g), peeled and chopped into 2cm chunks
1 tbsp olive oil
2 garlic cloves, peeled and thinly sliced
2–3 leeks (about 200–300g), trimmed, halved lengthways and finely chopped
1 heaped tbsp plain flour
400ml milk of choice
400g tin kidney beans, drained and rinsed (and roughly mashed up for babies)

For the crumble topping:
50g cold unsalted butter, cubed, or dairy-free spread
75g plain flour
20g porridge oats
15g Cheddar cheese, grated (optional)

Adaptations for the whole family: Serve your portion with lemony steamed greens.

1 Preheat the oven to 200°C/180°C fan.

2 In a medium roasting tray (about 20 x 30cm), add the sweet potato and drizzle with a little of the oil. Bake for 20 minutes.

3 Meanwhile, heat the remaining oil in a large saucepan over a medium-high heat. Add the garlic and leeks and cook for 15 minutes, stirring occasionally.

4 Stir in the flour, then add a splash of the milk and stir. Keep adding the milk gradually, stirring each time, until it thickens to a nice sauce.

5 Once the sweet potatoes are cooked, add these to the leek mix, along with the beans, and give it a good stir. Pop to one side while you make the topping. (Keep the roasting tray to hand as you will need it for the crumble.)

6 To make the crumble topping, in a bowl, add the butter and flour, and rub it between your fingers and thumbs to create chunky breadcrumbs.

7 Mix the oats and cheese (if using) into the crumble topping. Transfer the leek mix into the roasting tray, top with the crumble topping and bake for 25–30 minutes.

8 Scoop out a portion and give it a little mash for your baby, if needed, before serving.

Switching ingredients in/out: You can easily use plant-based milk if needed (I have made it with oat milk). Try using gluten-free flour and also a plant-based spread – they all work well.

Storing leftovers/how to defrost: Cool to room temperature within 2 hours. Place into an airtight container in the fridge and eat within 2 days. Alternatively, portion into batches and place in the freezer and consume within 3 months. Defrost in the fridge overnight or until fully thawed. Reheat until piping hot and then allow to cool before serving.

One-Pan Traffic Light Pasta

One-panners are so handy, especially now I have two children to feed and I need all the spare time I can get. This tasty recipe is super speedy, adds extra veggies and isn't so 'different' that it'll get rejected. If you're feeding a baby, you might want to chop up the spaghetti and veggies really well, or you could give it all a good mash when it's out of the pan. Spaghetti is always a great experimental one for babies and toddlers to try a new texture and practise their eating skills. If your little one isn't ready for it yet, chop, mash or swap spaghetti for another kind of pasta – it's your call!

Prep: 5–10 minutes
Cook: 12–15 minutes
Serves: 2 adults and 2 babies/toddlers, with leftovers

200g spaghetti (snapped into 5cm lengths to make it easier for toddlers to manage)
200g ripe medium tomatoes, finely chopped
50g coloured pepper, seeds and stalk removed, finely chopped
½ courgette (about 100g), coarsely grated
1 tsp olive oil
½ tbsp dried oregano
125g ricotta cheese
zest of 1 lemon and juice of ½

1 Add the spaghetti, tomatoes, pepper, courgette and 530 millilitres of water to a lidded shallow pan (about 30cm diameter). Pop the lid on and bring to the boil, reduce the heat and simmer for 5 minutes with the lid on. Remove the lid, give it a stir and add the oil and dried oregano.

2 Give it another stir and simmer, uncovered, for 8–10 minutes. You want the water to nearly all disappear, the pasta to be cooked and to be left with a yummy pasta sauce. (If the water is drying up and the pasta still needs longer to cook, add a few more splashes of water.)

3 Before serving, break up the ricotta cheese and add it to the pan, along with the lemon zest and juice. Stir to combine before serving.

Adaptations for the whole family: Season as required. Tomatoes are the only ingredient I do add a pinch of salt to for myself, so give this a go if it works for you.

Switching ingredients in/out: Swap the ingredients around if you need to use up other veg, such as carrots or broccoli, but you do need the tomatoes to help create the sauce.

Storing leftovers/how to defrost: Cool to room temperature within 2 hours. Place into an airtight container in the fridge and eat within 2 days. Alternatively, portion into batches without the ricotta and place in the freezer to consume within 3 months. Defrost in the fridge overnight or until fully thawed. Reheat until piping hot and then allow to cool before serving.

Mega Veg Curry

To my surprise, this is one of Ada's favourite recipes from the whole book and she asks for it regularly. It's such a quick and easy curry, and one that's now a staple in our house. It's a great way of exposing little ones to gentle flavours. Blend for younger babies and offer with some rice for texture or some bread to dip in. For younger kids, you might want to chop the aubergine and mushrooms really well as they can be tricky textures, but, as they get older, these are good ingredients to help them work on their eating skills.

Prep: 10 minutes
Cook: 15 minutes
Serves: 2 adult and 2 babies/toddlers, with leftovers

1 tbsp vegetable oil
½ red onion, peeled and finely chopped
1 tsp ground cinnamon
1 tsp ground cumin
1 small aubergine (about 200g), cut into 1cm chunks (or smaller for younger babies)
handful of chestnut mushrooms (about 100g), finely chopped
400g tin chopped tomatoes
½ x 400g tin green lentils, drained and rinsed

Switching ingredients in/out: Swap the aubergine for courgette or the mushrooms for carrot – whatever works for your family.

1. Heat the oil in a large non-stick saucepan over a medium heat. Add the onion, spices and aubergine. Cook for 5 minutes, stirring so it doesn't catch but colours nicely.

2. Add the mushrooms and keep cooking for another 5 minutes, stirring occasionally. Add the tomatoes and lentils and bring to the boil. Cook for a minute to warm through.

3. For babies, blend the curry to a puree before serving, if needed.

Serving ideas: Serve with rice or some flatbread cut into fingers for dunking.

Adaptations for the whole family: Leave the veg chunky for your portion if possible. Serve with a dollop of yoghurt and some nigella seeds on top. It's also lovely with some well-chopped dried apricot on top!

Storing leftovers/how to defrost: Cool to room temperature within 2 hours. Place into an airtight container in the fridge and eat within 2 days. Alternatively, portion into batches, place in the freezer and consume within 3 months. Defrost in the fridge overnight or until fully thawed. Reheat until piping hot and then allow to cool before serving.

 Tip: If your baby has never had aubergine before, they can have a 'contact reaction' to it sometimes (Ada did the first few times) and get a little rash around their mouth (see page 25). Don't panic if so – it's likely a skin reaction, not an immune reaction, if it's only in places the aubergine might have touched.

Rainbow Poke Bowl

This recipe looks beautiful, but it is also a little fiddly. However, each of the stages is super easy and you certainly get a colourful Instagram-worthy spread at the end. This is a fun one to do with little ones, getting them to help you prep some of the ingredients and assemble the finished dish. It's also a fab one to help with your little one's independence and building familiarity around food. When serving to babies, you might want to roll the rice into balls a little or give it a mash with a fork, and chop/mash or thinly slice the ingredients as needed, though I've made it suitable for most babies who have some experience with textures and finger foods. Leave off anything you're unsure about your baby being able to manage.

Prep: 15–20 minutes
Cook: 10 minutes
Serves: 2 adults and 2 babies/toddlers, with leftovers

2 corn on the cob
150g broccoli, chopped into small florets
400g cooked rice, such as sticky rice, brown basmati or wholegrain
150g cooked peeled prawns
75g cucumber, grated or cut into matchstick-thin slices
1 ripe avocado, peeled, stone removed and thinly sliced
150g pineapple or mango, cut into thin, soft slices (or use soft tinned pineapple)
2 free-range medium eggs, hard-boiled, sliced into rounds (thinly sliced for babies)
85g vacuum-packed beetroot, coarsely grated
1–2 tbsp sesame or onions seeds (optional)

For the dressing:
zest and juice of 2 limes
4 tbsp sesame oil

1   Bring a saucepan of water to the boil, add the corn on the cob and broccoli and cook for 10 minutes until the broccoli is soft and the corn on the cob cooked through. Drain and leave to one side. Once the corn on the cob is cooled, slice the corn off into thin 1cm slices.

2   Heat the rice according to the packet instructions.

3   To assemble the poke bowl, start by dividing the rice into four bowls, then top the rice with little sections of prawns, grated cucumber, mini broccoli florets, slices of corn on the cob, avocado slices, mango/pineapple slices, slices of egg, grated beetroot – however you fancy it … Allow your little ones to make their own, if they can, and add plenty of colour.

4   In a small bowl, make the dressing by mixing together the lime juice and sesame oil. Drizzle this over the bowls before serving. If you fancy, sprinkle with some sesame or onion seeds for extra flavour to finish.

Adaptations for the whole family: Add 1 tablespoon of soy sauce to the dressing for your portion.

Storing leftovers: Cool to room temperature within 1 hour. Place into an airtight container in the fridge and eat cold within 24 hours. Do not reheat pre-cooked microwave rice.

> **Tip:** You can use standard non-pre-cooked rice (around 200g) – just cook it according to the packet instructions.

Mixed Bean Casserole

This flavoursome casserole is packed with veggies and can be cooked in one pan, so it's a nice one for the slow cooker, or is just as easy on the hob. The veggies come out super soft, so it's an easy one to adapt the texture. It can be mashed or blended for smaller babies.

Prep: 10–15 minutes
Cook: 50–55 minutes
Serves: 2 adults and 2 babies/toddlers, with leftovers

1 tbsp olive oil
½ red or white onion, peeled and finely chopped
35g orange or yellow pepper, deseeded and cut into 2cm pieces
½ tbsp ground coriander
150g swede, peeled and cut into 2cm chunks
300g butternut squash, peeled and seeds removed, cut into 2cm chunks, or sweet potato, peeled and cut into 2cm chunks
handful of cauliflower (about 150g), cut into small florets
400g tin chopped tomatoes
400g tin mixed beans (in water – for example, black beans, pinto beans, haricot or chickpeas), drained and rinsed

1   Heat the oil in a large lidded casserole pan or non-stick saucepan over a medium-high heat.

2   Add the onion, pepper and ground coriander. Cook for 5 minutes, stirring occasionally.

3   Add the swede, butternut squash or sweet potato, cauliflower and tomatoes. Fill up the tomato tin halfway with water, swirl around and add to the pan. Give the casserole a good stir to mix it all together, then turn down the heat to medium and cook for 25 minutes with the lid on, stirring occasionally.

4   Add the beans and cook for another 20–25 minutes with the lid on, or until the veg is all cooked, stirring occasionally. Add a splash more water while cooking if it seems too dry.

5   Before serving, remove a few florets of cauliflower as finger foods, mash the beans a little for babies or blend the dish first.

Serving ideas: Serve with rice or couscous and the cauliflower florets on the side.

Storing leftovers/how to defrost: Cool to room temperature within 2 hours. Place into an airtight container in the fridge and eat within 2 days. Alternatively, portion into batches, place in the freezer and consume within 3 months. Defrost in the fridge overnight or until fully thawed. Reheat until piping hot and then allow to cool before serving.

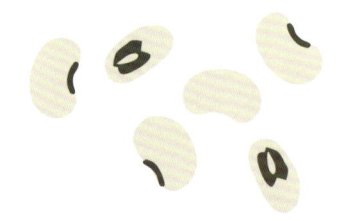

Mackerel Chowder

I like trying to introduce kids to lots of flavours and healthy ingredients nice and early on in their weaning journey, as we know that familiarity often leads to acceptance. Mackerel is quite a strong taste, so go easy on it in your baby's portion for the first few times of trying this recipe and add more as they get familiar with it. You might need to blend the sweetcorn for younger children. This is a lovely, hearty, warming recipe for the whole family!

Prep: 10 minutes
Cook: 25–30 minutes
Serves: 2 adults and 2 babies/toddlers, with leftovers

1 tbsp olive oil
1 white onion, peeled and finely chopped
1 tbsp plain flour
1 large white potato (about 160g), peeled for younger babies, cut into 1.5cm chunks
198g tin sweetcorn, drained
1–2 x 125g tins mackerel, in olive oil, drained
a few sprigs of dill or flat-leaf parsley, finely chopped
1 tbsp nutritional yeast
2 plain crackers, crumbled

1 Heat the oil in a large saucepan over a medium heat. Add the onion and cook for 8–10 minutes, or until it starts to turn golden, stirring occasionally.

2 Pop in the plain flour, give it a stir and then, little by little, add 650 millilitres of water, combining each time until it thickens.

3 Once you have added all the water, add in the potato and sweetcorn and simmer for at least 12 minutes (until the potatoes are soft). You can take out a portion for your baby at this stage and give it a good mash/blend, if needed.

4 Stir through the mackerel, breaking it up as you do, then stir in the dill or flat-leaf parsley and nutritional yeast.

5 Serve with the crackers crumbled on top.

Storing leftovers/how to defrost: Cool to room temperature within 2 hours. Place into an airtight container in the fridge and eat within 2 days. Alternatively, portion into batches and place in the freezer and consume within 3 months. Defrost in the fridge overnight or until fully thawed. Reheat until piping hot and then allow to cool before serving.

Easy Peasy Shepherds Piesy

I love a shepherd's pie, but I don't love the faff that comes with it and so actively avoid doing them too much! This is a super quick veggie version, using sliced potatoes and frozen veg to make it in half the time. It's really tasty and makes enough for a family with some leftovers, so you can have a nice hearty meal for another day too. You might want to give it all a good mash or a blend for younger babies, but the textures are really soft here and the thin potatoes can work well as finger foods too!

Prep: 10 minutes
Cook: 55–60 minutes
Serves: 2 adults and 2 babies/ toddlers, with leftovers

1 tbsp olive oil, plus extra
   for drizzling
1 white onion, peeled and
   finely chopped
250g frozen veg mix (peas/
   sweetcorn/broccoli)
2 tbsp tomato puree
1 tbsp plain flour
400–500ml hot water or
   low-salt stock
400g tin lentils, drained
   and rinsed
300g potatoes
50g Cheddar cheese, grated

Switching ingredients in/out:
Use gluten-free flour if needed and leave out the cheese or use a dairy-free alternative.

1 Heat the oil in a large saucepan over a medium heat. Add the onion and cook for 8 minutes, stirring occasionally.

2 Preheat the oven 200°C/180°C fan.

3 Add the frozen veg to the pan and cook for a further 5 minutes, then add the tomato puree and flour and give it a good stir. Gradually add in the water or stock, stirring each time you add some until it thickens (this can take some time). Once thickened, pop in the lentils and then bring to the boil. Cook for 1 minute to warm through, then turn off the heat.

4 Carefully transfer the veggie mix to an ovenproof dish/tin (about 20 x 25cm).

5 Slice the potatoes very thinly and lay the slices over the top of the veggie mix, slightly overlapping to completely cover the pie.

6 Drizzle with a little olive oil and cook in the oven for 20 minutes. Remove from the oven, sprinkle over the cheese and pop back in the oven for a final 20 minutes. Leave to cool before serving.

Serving ideas: Serve as it is or with a side of greens, if you prefer.

Adaptations for the whole family: This is delicious as it is, though you might want to season your portion if you use water instead of stock.

Storing leftovers/how to defrost: Cool to room temperature within 2 hours. Place into an airtight container in the fridge and eat within 2 days. Alternatively, portion into batches, place in the freezer and consume within 3 months. Defrost in the fridge overnight or until fully thawed. Reheat until piping hot and then allow to cool before serving.

Megamix Pasta Salad

Offering different and more complex textures to babies can be a real winner for helping them to learn to eat, and this one is definitely a bit of a challenging texture, with some raw grated veggies. It's probably best for older babies who are experienced with plenty of textures, but you can always give bits a mash before offering to younger babies. I love quirky dishes like this which combine fruit and veg with other savoury flavours. You can leave out the dairy (and the nuts) if you prefer. My family loves this and I've also brought it out at a few picnics and parties too as it's quick, easy and a bit of an all-rounder.

Prep: 10 minutes
Cook: 6–8 minutes (grains/pasta depending)
Serves: 2 adults and 2 babies/toddlers, with leftovers

200g giant couscous/orzo or bow pasta
½ courgette (about 200g), grated
120g strawberries, hulled and cut into thin matchsticks
1 carrot (about 80g), coarsely grated

For the dressing:
large handful of basil, leaves picked and very finely chopped
½–1 small garlic clove, peeled and crushed
2–3 tbsp olive oil
1–2 tbsp Greek yoghurt or dairy-free alternative (optional)
juice of ½ lemon
25g ground nuts (for example, almonds, pistachios or pine nuts) (optional)

1 Cook the grains/pasta according to the packet instructions. Drain and rinse in cold water, then set to one side.

2 Meanwhile, in a large bowl, add the courgette, strawberries and carrot. Mix together and then add the cooled grains/pasta.

3 To make the dressing, either mix all the ingredients in a bowl or pop it all into a blender and blitz until smooth and combined. If you are using the nuts, you might need a splash or two more of the oil to loosen the mix.

4 Add the dressing to the salad bowl and give it a final good mix before serving. Alternatively, you could just use a small drizzle of the sauce on your baby's portion as it has some strong flavours in it.

Serving ideas: This works well served on its own as a light and refreshing meal, but is also delicious served alongside some cooked chicken or fish.

Adaptations for the whole family: Try adding some grilled halloumi to your portion.

Storing leftovers: Place into an airtight container in the fridge and eat within 2 days.

Veggie Open Tart

This is such an easy recipe that works for a quick lunch or dinner, or even as a snack, for any member of the family. It's also super easy to adapt: use whatever greens you have left in the fridge and, if you prefer, pop some grated cheese on top at the end of cooking. Of course, you can use pastry if you prefer, but I love the ease and simplicity of this one and pastry can be quite high in salt and saturated fat.

Prep: 10 minutes
Cook: 30–36 minutes
Makes: 1 tart

oil, for greasing
1–3 large wholemeal wraps
4 large free-range eggs, whisked
50ml milk of choice
handful of greens (about 40g), such as spinach, broccoli, asparagus or other leafy greens, washed and shredded or finely chopped, plus a few extra asparagus spears (optional), to decorate
50g sweet potatoes, coarsely grated
small handful of herbs (for example, chives or flat-leaf parsley), leaves picked and finely chopped (optional)

1   Preheat the oven to 200°C/180°C fan.

2   Grease a 20cm round loose-bottomed tart tin with a little oil. Line the tin with one wrap so that it acts like your base layer (and flaps over the edges slightly). You might need more wraps to cover the whole bottom of the tin depending on its size and shape.

3   Into a large bowl or jug, add the eggs, milk, greens and sweet potato. Mix until combined.

4   Pop the tin onto a baking tray, then carefully pour in the egg mix, sprinkle over the herbs (if using) and decorate with a few extra asparagus tips (if using).

5   Cover with foil and pop into the oven for 6 minutes. Then remove the foil and bake for another 25–30 minutes, or until the egg is cooked through and the wrap is nice and golden on top. Check the tart halfway through and, if it is starting to brown too much, just pop the foil back on top.

6   Leave to cool for 10–15 minutes, then carefully run a palette knife around the sides of the tart case, remove the tart to a board and serve cut into wedges or little finger shape sticks for baby.

Serving ideas: Serve with a nice fresh lemony salad (see page 191).

Adaptations for the whole family: Sprinkle some crumbled feta cheese over your portion before serving.

Storing leftovers/how to defrost: Cool to room temperature within 2 hours. Place into an airtight container in the fridge and eat within 2 days. Alternatively, portion into airtight containers, place in the freezer and consume within 3 months. Defrost in the fridge overnight or until fully thawed. Reheat until piping hot and then allow to cool before serving.

Image overleaf →

Tip: For young babies the tortilla might be a little tricky to manage once hard, so chop off the edges of this 'tart' before offering to baby so they get the wrap underneath and the eggy mixture.

Mini Meatloaves and Mash

This is a bit of a different recipe for me, but it's super easy and a mix between meatballs and a meatloaf (but mini, so fab for kids). Combined with the broccoli mash, it's a great way to get extra veg in. It also has a super quick gravy which is great for dunking the meatloaves in.

Prep: 5 minutes
Cook: 35–45 minutes
Serves: 2 adults and 2 babies/toddlers, with leftovers

1 tbsp olive oil
2 red onions, peeled and finely diced
6 sprigs of fresh thyme, leaves picked
500g turkey mince
1 tsp ground cinnamon
1 tbsp dried oregano
handful of homemade or shop-bought dried breadcrumbs
450g potatoes, peeled and chopped into 2cm chunks
130g broccoli, trimmed, stalk thinly sliced and florets roughly chopped
1 tbsp plain flour
250–400ml hot water or low-salt stock
20g mature Cheddar, grated
knob of unsalted butter or dairy-free spread (optional)

1 Preheat the oven 200°C/180°C fan. Line a baking tray with greaseproof paper.

2 Heat 1 tablespoon of the oil in a medium frying pan over a medium heat. Add the onions and cook for 5 minutes, stirring occasionally. Add the thyme leaves and cook for a further 2 minutes.

3 Add half of the cooked onion and thyme mix to a bowl along with the turkey mince, cinnamon, oregano and breadcrumbs. Keep the other half in the frying pan and take off the heat, leaving to one side to make a gravy later. Use your hands to mix the turkey mince and the other ingredients together.

4 Shape into 6–8 thick sausage/mini meatloaf shapes (approximately 8cm long).

5 Pop the meatloaves onto the lined tray, drizzle with a little oil and cook in the oven for 20–25 minutes.

6 Meanwhile, bring a small saucepan of water to the boil, add the potatoes and cook for 10–15 minutes until soft, adding the broccoli for the final 5–7 minutes. Once the potatoes and broccoli have cooked, drain and leave to steam-dry for 5 minutes.

7 While you're waiting, make the gravy. Pop the frying pan back over a medium heat, add the other half of the onion and thyme mix along with the flour and stir to make a paste. Then gradually add the water or stock a little at a time, whisking/mixing until thickened each time. Cook for 10–15 minutes, stirring continually to avoid lumps forming.

8 Return the potatoes and broccoli to the saucepan, add the cheese and butter (if using), and mash until smooth.

9 Serve the mini meatloaves with the mash and the gravy poured over the top.

Tip: To make your own breadcrumbs, just whizz up ½ slice of good-quality bread (wholemeal if possible) in a blender or food processor. These mini meatloaves can be served without gravy, or feel free to use standard low-salt gravy granules.

Adaptations for the whole family: Add a little mustard to your gravy for a kick and season to taste if you used water instead of stock.

Storing leftovers/how to defrost: Cool to room temperature within 2 hours. Place into an airtight container in the fridge and eat within 2 days. Alternatively, place in the freezer and consume within 3 months. Defrost in the fridge overnight or until fully thawed. Reheat until piping hot and then allow to cool before serving.

Speedy Stir Fry with Tofu Strips

This super speedy stir fry packs in a lot of flavour for little ones. It might be a bit more challenging for younger babies to eat, but once they are experienced with finger foods, try offering them the soft cooked veggies and noodles separately on a plate and let them explore it all. You could also try offering the sauce on the side for them as a 'dipping sauce'. Grate the carrot and courgette for younger babies if it's easier for them to eat this way, but the ribbons are fab for older kids to explore. If you want to use chicken instead of the tofu you can.

Prep: 5 minutes
Cook: 10–15 minutes
Serves: 2 adults and 2 babies/ toddlers, with leftovers

135g rice noodles
2 tbsp toasted sesame oil
1½ tbsp smooth peanut butter
2 tbsp hot water
2 garlic cloves, peeled and crushed
zest and juice of 1 lime
1 carrot (about 150g), peeled
1 courgette (about 200g), ends trimmed
280g extra-firm tofu or free-range skinless and boneless chicken breast, cut into 1cm strips
large handful of frozen peas or green beans (about 100g)
small handful of coriander leaves, finely chopped (optional)

1 Cook the noodles according to the packet instructions. Drain and rinse in cold water, then set to one side.

2 In a bowl, add 1 tablespoon of the sesame oil, the peanut butter, hot water, garlic and lime zest and juice. Give it a good mix and leave to one side.

3 Using a vegetable peeler, shave the carrot and courgette into long thin ribbons, or grate them if serving to younger babies.

4 Heat the remaining oil in a wok or large frying pan over a high heat. Add the tofu and stir-fry for 5–8 minutes, stirring occasionally so it starts to get golden all over. If using chicken, stir-fry for 10 minutes until browned all over and cooked through. Move the tofu or chicken to one side of the pan, then add the carrot, courgette, peas or green beans and cook for another 5 minutes (give the peas a little mash for younger babies).

5 Pour in the peanut dressing and noodles, and give it a good mix to combine. Keep on the heat for a minute, then stir in the coriander (if using) before serving.

Adaptations for the whole family: Add a splash of soy sauce, some chopped peanuts and chilli sauce to your portion before serving if you like. For older children, use some scissors to give it a bit of a chop and let them tuck in.

Storing leftovers: Cool to room temperature within 2 hours. Place into an airtight container in the fridge and eat within 2 days. Reheat until piping hot and then allow to cool before serving.

Simple Cod Traybake

In most of my books I've done a fish traybake and they've always gone down *so* well. My Prawn, Pepper and Kidney Bean Nacho Traybake and Creamy Lemony Salmon Bake have been two of my most loved recipes, so I wanted to include another one in this book! This is a really fresh and flavourful dish and is super simple. It's also so easy to adapt for a baby as needed – just mash it all together with a few sticks of greens on the side or offer the elements as single items for your baby to feed themselves. For older toddlers, just let them explore as they need.

Prep: 5 minutes
Cook: 35–40 minutes
Serves: 2 adults and 2 babies/
toddlers, with leftovers

3 medium sweet potatoes
   (about 750g), peeled and
   chopped into 2cm chunks
200g greens (such as asparagus
   spears, green beans or
   broccoli florets)
½ tbsp olive oil
3–4 cod fillets (about 375–500g)
½ tsp ground turmeric

For the dressing:
1.5cm piece of fresh ginger,
   peeled and grated
juice of 1 lemon
1 tbsp olive oil

1   Preheat the oven to 200°C/180°C fan.

2   Add the sweet potatoes and greens to a medium roasting tray (about 20 x 30cm) and drizzle with the oil. Give it a mix around to coat the potato, then pop in the oven for 20 minutes.

3   Meanwhile, make the dressing. In a bowl, add the ginger, lemon juice and oil. Give it a good stir and leave to one side.

4   Remove the tray from the oven and add the cod fillets. Sprinkle the turmeric and drizzle the zingy dressing over the cod and cook for a further 15–20 minutes. Keep an eye on the greens towards the end of the cooking time and remove any from the oven if they are starting to char. You want them to be soft and well cooked but not too brown.

5   Before serving, flake up the cod and mash any veg that needs it for babies.

Storing leftovers: Cool to room temperature within 2 hours. Place into an airtight container in the fridge and eat within 2 days. Reheat until piping hot and then allow to cool before serving.

'Use Up the Leftovers' Veggie Sauce

The idea behind this recipe is for you to use whatever veggies you have to hand, blend it all together and then use it as a 'sauce' base for making anything else you want. I haven't added any flavours to allow you to adapt and make it versatile when you're adding extras. For example, use it on top of jacket potatoes with a bit of cheese, blend it (or leave it chunky) and serve with some pasta, add some mixed beans and make it into a chilli with some spices, or chop some fresh tomatoes and add them to it to make a salsa for fajitas or tacos … you name it, make it yours!

Prep: 10–15 minutes
Cook: 30 minutes
Serves: 2 adults and 2 babies/toddlers, with leftovers

1 tbsp olive oil
around 500g leftover raw veggies, including: onions, carrots, celery, leeks, pepper, butternut squash, all finely chopped
1 garlic clove, peeled and crushed
2 x 400g tins chopped or plum tomatoes
400g tin beans (such as borlotti, butter or kidney), drained and rinsed (optional)

1   Heat the oil in a large lidded non-stick saucepan over a medium heat. Add all the veggies and the garlic, stir together and cook for 15 minutes, stirring occasionally.

2   Add the tomatoes, a tin of water (400ml) and the beans (if using), and stir to combine.

3   Put the lid on the pan and continue cooking for 15 minutes, stirring occasionally.

4   Mash or blend the beans for smaller babies and use the sauce for whatever recipe you have planned!

Adaptations for the whole family: Add a little spice to your portion by adding some chopped red chilli before serving or fry off some capers for a little salty crunch!

Storing leftovers/how to defrost: Cool to room temperature within 2 hours. Place into an airtight container in the fridge and eat within 2 days. Alternatively, portion into batches for different uses, place in the freezer and consume within 3 months. Defrost in the fridge overnight or until fully thawed. Reheat until piping hot and then allow to cool before serving.

Leek and Tomato Pasta Bake

This is a fab dish for when you have little prep time, but want a warming and simple dinner as it can be thrown into one pan and pretty much left alone. I really like using leeks in recipes as I think they pack in flavour and are a little different too. They can be a strong flavour for babies, though, so do feel free to use one leek and simply grate in some courgette in place of the second leek. Depending on the size of your pasta, give it a little mash before offering it to your baby and keep aside a few whole pieces of the pasta shape as finger foods.

Prep: 10 minutes
Cook: 40 minutes
Serves: 2 adults and 2 babies/ toddlers, with leftovers

1 garlic clove, peeled and crushed
1–2 leeks (about 200–300g), trimmed, halved lengthways and thinly sliced
1 white or red onion, peeled and finely chopped
300g pasta shapes (such as fusilli, farfalle or penne – whatever you fancy!)
400g tin chopped tomatoes
drizzle of olive oil
½ x 400g tin beans (such as borlotti, haricot or butter beans), drained and rinsed (mashed for babies)
65g Cheddar cheese, grated

1 Preheat the oven to 200°C/180°C fan.

2 Add the garlic, leeks, onion, dried pasta, tomatoes and 500 millilitres of water to a large roasting tray (about 25 x 30cm). Stir, drizzle with the oil, cover with foil and cook for 30 minutes.

3 Remove the foil then pour in the beans and give it all a mix. Sprinkle over the cheese and pop it back in the oven, uncovered, for 10 minutes. When the cheese has melted and it looks lovely and golden, then it's ready to serve up.

Adaptations for the whole family: Add some extra cheese, if you like, and season to taste.

Switching ingredients in/out: Swap the beans for another protein like beef mince, if you prefer, but you might need to add it a little earlier in the recipe to give it enough time to cook through.

Storing leftovers/how to defrost: Cool to room temperature within 2 hours. Place into an airtight container in the fridge and eat within 2 days. Reheat until piping hot and then allow to cool before serving.

Tip: You could use the other half of the tin of beans in the Veg Soup recipe on page 138.

Baby's First 'Salad'

I love a side salad, especially one with a really simple and tasty dressing that can also be offered to little ones. This is such an easy option and you can add or remove the extras to make it even simpler. It's a great one for exploring more finger foods with your baby too, though they might need a fair amount of finger food experience before they go in for this meal as there are lots of variable textures in this salad.

Prep: 10 minutes
Cook: 10 minutes
Serves: 2 adults and 2 babies/toddlers as a main, or plenty as a side salad

100g cucumber, halved and cut into thin matchsticks
100g ripe medium tomatoes, thinly sliced
1 little gem lettuce, halved and shredded
50g vacuum-packed beetroot in natural juices, drained and coarsely grated
75g stale bread, cut into strips (optional)
1 tbsp extra-virgin olive oil, plus an extra drizzle for the croutons (if using)
1 tbsp fresh lemon juice
170g firm tofu or cooked chicken breast, cut into thin strips (optional)

1   If serving with croutons, preheat the oven to 200°C/180°C fan.

2   Pop the cucumber, tomatoes, little gem and beetroot into a salad bowl. Give it all a good mix then pop to one side.

3   Place the strips of bread (if using) onto a baking tray and drizzle with a little oil. Bake for 10 minutes until golden and crispy.

4   In the salad bowl, add the oil and lemon juice. Give it a good mix, adding in the tofu or chicken (if using).

5   Serve up by crumbling over a few croutons as a crunchy topping.

Serving ideas: Serve alongside another meal as an extra side salad or lay the different strips of veggies/bread/meats out for younger babies to help themselves to as finger foods.

Adaptations for the whole family: Season your portion well and add in some crumbled feta cheese. Or crush ½–1 whole garlic clove and add it to the adult portions with the dressing. Older children might want to try the lettuce in bigger pieces.

Storing leftovers: Will keep in the fridge for 1–2 days in an airtight container. Store the leftover croutons in a separate container to stop them getting soggy.

Tip: Use premade croutons if you prefer (though check for added salt) and shop-bought cooked chicken strips work well too. The rest ideally needs to be fresh!

Baby's First Roast

There is no reason why your little one can't take part in your family roast dinners early on in their weaning journey. Some of the veggies (if cooked well) are perfect for little ones experimenting with finger foods. This recipe makes a low-salt gravy, though you can use standard gravy for your portion if you prefer. Save any excess gravy and use it with the Mini Meatloaves on page 182.

Prep: 10–15 minutes
Cook: 50–60 minutes
Serves: 2 adults and
2 babies/toddlers

350g new potatoes, cut into
   halves
a few sprigs of thyme
1 garlic clove, peeled and crushed
1 tbsp olive oil
1 red or white onion, peeled and
   cut into 10 wedges
2 medium carrots, peeled and
   thinly sliced on an angle
2–3 free-range skinless and
   boneless chicken breasts
   (about 450g in total)
300g greens (for example, peas,
   broccoli or green beans),
   chopped

For the gravy:
1 tbsp plain flour
½ tbsp garlic powder
550ml hot water

Adaptations for the whole family: Use standard gravy for your own portion if you prefer and for older children; just avoid adding too much gravy for younger children and babies as it's quite high in salt.

1   Preheat the oven to 220°C/200°C fan.

2   In a large roasting tray (about 25 x 30cm), add the potatoes, keeping them to one side of the tray. Top with the sprigs of thyme and the garlic, and drizzle with half the oil. On the other side of the tray, add the onion wedges and half of the carrots. Put the tray into the middle of the oven and cook for 20 minutes.

3   Score the surface of the chicken breasts a few times and add them to the tray, making space among the vegetables. Drizzle with the rest of the oil and cook for a further 20–25 minutes until the chicken is cooked through.

4   Meanwhile, bring a saucepan of water to the boil and add the remaining carrots and the greens and cook for 10 minutes, adding the peas for the final 3 minutes.

5   To make the gravy, remove the potatoes and chicken breast from the tray and pop to one side, covered, or place on another tray and leave in a low oven to keep warm but not cook anymore.

6   Add the flour and garlic powder to the tray with the roasted onion and carrots (or add everything to a saucepan, including the sticky bits from the tray), pop it on a low heat on the hob and start stirring, then slowly add a little of the water, mixing to form a nice paste. Keep adding the water and stirring to get all the sticky bits off the side of the tray – this will give you loads of great flavour – until you have a nice consistency. You can sieve the gravy at this stage or keep the chunky veg bits in – it's up to you! (Sieve the gravy for babies or blend it to make a thicker gravy.)

7   Serve the gravy alongside the rest of the roast, slicing the chicken for babies and flattening the peas (if using), for younger babies.

Storing leftovers/how to defrost: Cool to room temperature within 2 hours. Place the gravy and chicken/veg in separate airtight containers in the fridge and eat within 2 days. Alternatively, place in the freezer and consume within 3 months. Defrost in the fridge overnight. Reheat until piping hot and allow to cool before serving.

Mushroom and Chickpea Stew

This is a lovely one to make in bulk and serve in lots of different ways for babies and toddlers. I love mushrooms and they aren't always an ingredient that you see much in toddler cookbooks, but they offer a unique flavour and texture. One of Ada's favourite foods for a while was mushrooms, so I have a lot of mushroom recipes in my books and blog. Make sure you mash the chickpeas for little ones and also give the mushrooms a really good chop, as the slimy texture of them once cooked can be a little challenging for new eaters! You can easily blend this one for younger babies too – it gives a fab flavour, and you can add it on toast or serve with potatoes or rice.

Prep: 10 minutes
Cook: 18–20 minutes
Serves: 2 adults and 2 babies/ toddlers, with leftovers

drizzle of olive oil
2 garlic cloves, peeled and crushed
3 sprigs of thyme, leaves picked
300g mushrooms, finely chopped
10 cherry tomatoes, finely chopped
200g couscous
400g tin chickpeas, drained and rinsed
2 heaped tbsp full-fat cream cheese or dairy-free alternative
small handful of flat-leaf parsley, finely chopped (optional)

1   In a large frying pan, add the oil, garlic and thyme. Cook over a medium heat for 2–3 minutes, or until starting to get a bit of colour.

2   Add the mushrooms and tomatoes and cook for 10–12 minutes, stirring occasionally.

3   Meanwhile, cook the couscous according to the packet instructions and leave to the side.

4   Add the chickpeas to the frying pan, along with 100 millilitres of water and the cream cheese or dairy-free alternative. Give it a good stir to combine the sauce.

5   Bring to the boil and stir through the chopped parsley (if using) before serving in a bowl alongside the couscous for your baby to self-feed. If offering to a younger baby, blend or give it a good mash first.

Adaptations for the whole family: Add some extra herbs to the top of your portion.

Storing leftovers/how to defrost: Cool to room temperature within 2 hours. Place into an airtight container in the fridge and eat within 2 days. Alternatively, portion into batches, place in the freezer and consume within 3 months. Defrost in the fridge overnight or until fully thawed. Reheat until piping hot and then allow to cool before serving.

Hotpot with Herby Dumplings

This one's a really hearty meal for the whole family and can easily be done in a slow cooker. The herby dumplings add quite a bit of extra flavour and texture, and they are fab for little babies to munch on. They can get a little gloopy, so chop them smaller if needed for younger babies or toddlers. If you don't fancy making the dumplings, just pop in some new potatoes and cook with the stew for 15–20 minutes.

Prep: 10 minutes
Cook: 2 hours 20 minutes (or 1 hour 10 minutes if using kidney beans)
Serves: 2 adults and 2 babies/toddlers, with leftovers

drizzle of olive oil
400g stewing beef fillet, cut into bite-sized pieces, or 400g tin kidney beans, drained and rinsed
1 white onion, peeled and roughly chopped
1 garlic clove, peeled and crushed
2 large carrots, chopped into 1cm chunks
1–2 sprigs of rosemary or thyme
1 tbsp tomato puree
1 tbsp plain flour
1 medium parsnip, peeled and chopped into 1cm chunks
1 litre hot water

For the dumplings:
70g cold unsalted butter, cut into cubes
135g self-raising flour
1 tbsp fresh thyme, leaves picked and finely chopped

1 Heat the oil in a large casserole pan over a medium heat. Add the beef and cook for 10 minutes until browned on all sides. (Skip this step if using kidney beans.)

2 Add the onion, garlic, carrot and whole rosemary/thyme sprigs to the pan. Continue cooking for a further 10 minutes, stirring occasionally.

3 Add the tomato puree and flour, mix to combine, then add the parsnip and water. Give it another good mix. (Add the kidney beans now if using instead of the beef.)

4 Bring to the boil, then cover, turn down to a simmer and cook for 2 hours, or until the beef is cooked and falling apart easily. (If using kidney beans, cook for around an hour, until the veggies are nice and soft.)

5 Meanwhile, make the herby dumplings. In a bowl, add the butter and flour, and rub it between your fingers and thumbs to create breadcrumbs. Stir in the herbs, then slowly add 70 millilitres of cold water to form a dough. Add a little more flour if needed.

6 Roll the mix into 12 balls (this is slightly easier if your hands are a little wet), then pop them in the fridge to keep cold.

7 Carefully add the dumplings to the pan 20 minutes before the cooking time is up. The dumplings should be puffed up and cooked through before serving.

8 Serve in a bowl, mashing down the veggies/beans and shredding the beef for babies, if needed (you can remove the dumplings and blend the stew a little if you need to before offering to younger babies).

Storing leftovers/how to defrost: Cool to room temperature within 2 hours. Place into an airtight container in the fridge and eat within 2 days. Alternatively, freeze in batches and separate the dumplings into another container, place in the freezer and consume within 3 months. If using potatoes instead of dumplings, no need to separate. Defrost in the fridge overnight or until fully thawed. Reheat until piping hot and then allow to cool before serving.

Celebration Foods

I always try to include a celebration section in my books, and this one is no exception. For me, foods that we bring out to celebrate different occasions don't all need to be salty and sweet.

Of course, if you want to offer your little ones standard sweetened cakes and party food, that's perfectly OK, but these recipes are here to give you delicious and birthday-spread-worthy alternative versions with lower levels of those nutrients that kids don't need so much of in their diets. My favourites are the Cinnamon Crunch Carrot Cakes, No Added Sugar Chocolate Mousse and Chickpea Mini 'Sausage' Rolls. I can't wait for you to try them.

Fruit Cocktail and Ginger Sponge Traybake

Traybakes can be a really handy option to whip out at celebration occasions as well as for breakfasts or on-the-go snacks. This one might vary, depending on the type of fruit cocktail mix you get and the flavours and fruits in it. Give any big bits or whole grapes a chop up before you mix it in, if needed, but the cocktail mix adds a fab flavour to this traybake and the fruits generally come out very soft.

Prep: 10 minutes
Cook: 25–30 minutes
Makes: 8–10 portions
(for adults and kids!)

140g unsalted butter, softened and chopped into cubes, or plant-based spread
1 large banana (about 120g), peeled and mashed
2 large free-range eggs or 2 flaxseed eggs (see page 40)
zest of 1 orange
170g self-raising flour
½ tsp ground ginger
415g tin fruit cocktail mix in juice or 415g tinned pears, drained (chopped or sliced if needed)
Greek yoghurt, to serve (optional)

1. Preheat the oven to 200°C/180°C fan. Line an ovenproof dish (around 20 x 20cm) with greaseproof paper.

2. In a bowl, use a hand whisk to mix the butter and mashed banana together. Add the eggs and orange zest, give it a good mix, then stir in the flour and ground ginger. Add the tinned fruit and give it another mix. Pour it into the dish and spread it out on top, roughly.

3. Pop it in the oven and bake for 25–30 minutes, or until cooked through and golden.

4. Let it cool a little in the dish, then remove to a cooling rack to cool a little more. Cut into little finger sticks for younger babies and make sure there are no big pieces of fruit. Slice into bigger squares for older toddlers or adults and serve with a dollop of Greek yoghurt, if using.

Adaptations for the whole family: Add a drizzle of honey to your portion when serving.

Storing leftovers/how to defrost: Will keep at room temperature in an airtight container, in the fridge for 2 days or in the freezer for up to 3 months. Thoroughly defrost in the fridge overnight before serving.

Giant Pancake Cake

I love coming up with ideas for low- or no-sugar celebration cakes that make birthdays for little ones seem special. I've included a birthday cake-style recipe in each of my books to date and wanted to feature the pancake cake I made for Raffy for his second birthday in this one. The idea for this cake is based on a flat sheet pancake recipe, where you simply add some sweeter fruits to the mix and turn them into a cake with some filling. It's not a sweet cake by any means, as it has no added sugar (unless you use the icing sugar on top), but it looks fab and babies and toddlers love it!

Prep: 10 minutes
Cook: 20–25 minutes
Makes: 8–10 slices
(for adults and kids!)

unsalted butter or plant-based
   spread, for greasing
250g self-raising flour
1 tsp baking powder
1 large free-range egg
300ml milk of choice
150g frozen cherries/berries,
   defrosted
icing sugar, for dusting
   (optional)

For the filling:
300g Greek yoghurt or
   dairy-free alternative
1 tsp vanilla bean paste
   or extract

1   Line 2 x 18cm loose-bottomed cake tins with greaseproof paper on the base and grease the sides. Preheat the oven to 200°C/180°C fan.

2   Sift the flour and baking powder into a bowl, then make a well in the middle.

3   In a separate jug, crack the egg and whisk it together with the milk. Add the milk mixture to the well in the middle of the flour bowl and whisk the whole mixture together until you have a smooth batter.

4   Divide the batter between the two cake tins and then drop in the cherries/berries and roughly mix through. Cook for 20–25 minutes (or until golden on top and cooked through).

5   Once cooked, remove from the tins to a cooling rack.

6   To make the filling, mix together the Greek yoghurt and vanilla bean paste or extract in a bowl. Spread it into the middle of one of the cakes then pop the other one on top.

7   Dust the top with icing sugar (if you fancy it!).

Adaptations for the whole family: Add some sugar into the dry mix or use a sweeter filling such as buttercream icing or jam and cream for your portion as this really isn't a sweet option for those who are used to standard cakes!

Storing leftovers/how to defrost: Will keep in the fridge for 2 days, in airtight container. Freeze the pancakes without the yoghurt filling in an airtight container with baking paper between for up to 3 months. Defrost in the fridge overnight.

Mini Veggie Muffins

I'm a *huge* fan of tasty muffins that don't need the added salt and sugars we usually see. You can add lots of flavour with basic, healthy ingredients and a really delicious mix of green ingredients goes into these savoury muffins. These are a new firm favourite in our household.

Prep: 15 minutes
Cook: 25 minutes
Makes: 12–14 mini muffins

200g coarsely grated courgette
50g frozen peas, defrosted
handful of mint, leaves picked
   and roughly chopped
   (optional)
1 large free-range egg, whisked
50g oil or unsalted butter,
   melted
175ml milk of choice
225g self-raising flour
1 tsp garlic powder
50g Cheddar or Parmesan
   cheese, grated

1   Preheat the oven to 200°C/180°C fan. Line two 12-hole cupcake or muffin tins with cases (you'll need 14 cases in total).

2   In a large mixing bowl, add the courgette, peas and mint (if using). Then add the egg, oil (or melted butter) and milk. Give it all a good mix.

3   Stir in the flour, garlic powder and cheese.

4   Divide the batter between the 12–14 cases and bake for 25 minutes, or until golden and cooked through.

5   Remove to a cooling rack and leave to cool completely before serving.

Adaptations for the whole family: Add a little extra cheese into your half of the mix and enjoy with a cup of tea.

Storing leftovers/how to defrost: Store in an airtight container in the fridge for 2 days or in the freezer for up to 3 months. Allow to thoroughly defrost in the fridge overnight before serving.

Chickpea Mini 'Sausage' Rolls

This is one of my favourite recipes in the whole of this book! I love pastry foods, but don't use them too often for little ones as they can be quite salty and high in saturated fats. However, this makes a delicious and nutrient-filled snack or party food option – if you don't eat them all before the party starts, that is! As with some of my other recipes, if you can't find no added salt curry powder, you can use standard curry powder – just be mindful of how much you use in your baby's portion.

Prep: 15 minutes
Cook: 25–30 minutes
Makes: 20 mini rolls

1 tsp olive oil
1 onion, peeled and finely chopped
½ tsp ground cumin
½ tsp no added salt mild curry powder
½ tsp ground coriander
400g tin chickpeas, drained and rinsed
150g fresh tomatoes, finely chopped
4 dried apricots (about 30g), finely chopped
320g puff pastry sheet
A little milk of choice
2 tsp poppy seeds

Serving ideas: Serve these with a side of veggie sticks or just have them as they are on the go.

Tip: Use frozen diced onions to make things easier. Give the mixture a pulse in a blender instead of mashing.

1   Preheat the oven to 210°C/190°C fan. Line two baking trays with greaseproof paper.

2   Heat the oil in a medium frying pan over a medium-high heat, add the onion and spices and cook for 5 minutes. Add the chickpeas and tomatoes, turn the heat down to medium and cook for another 5 minutes, stirring occasionally.

3   Remove from the heat and thoroughly mash the chickpeas into the spice mix, then stir in the apricots. Put to one side.

4   Lay out the pastry sheet horizontally on a clean surface. Cut across the middle horizontally (across the longest length) so you have 2 strips about 10cm wide. Carefully divide the mixture along the middle of each strip (you will be folding it over and sealing it, so make sure you leave a little 1cm gap around all edges).

5   Brush the edges with the milk and carefully fold over the top half to meet the bottom half lengthways to enclose the filling in the pastry. Using a fork, seal the cut edges, brush with the milk, cut into 4cm rolls and sprinkle with poppy seeds.

6   Pop onto the lined trays and bake for 15–20 minutes, or until golden.

7   Allow to cool before serving to little ones as they come out very hot.

Adaptations for the whole family: These are perfect as they are, but you could add a little sweet chilli sauce and a crunchy salad on the side.

Storing leftovers/how to defrost: Store in an airtight container in the fridge for 2 days or in the freezer for up to 3 months. Allow to thoroughly defrost in the fridge overnight. Heat through until piping hot and then allow to cool before serving.

Image overleaf →

No Added Sugar Chocolate Mousse

This is such a delicious explosion for the taste buds and feels very special. I'm so chuffed with this recipe and think little ones (and adults) will love it. It's perfect for parties (double up the recipe if you need to make more) and for special occasions too, but, because it's easy to make and contains a lot of nutrients, you can bring it out whenever. It's quite rich, so you don't need huge portions – a few teaspoons will usually do!

Prep: 5 minutes
Serves: 2 adults and 1–2 babies/toddlers

100g dried dates (Medjool if possible), destoned and roughly torn
150g Greek yoghurt or dairy-free alternative
2 tsp cocoa powder
zest of 1 large orange
sprinkle of my Super Duper Seed Mix (see page 125, optional)

1 Pop the dates, yoghurt and cocoa powder into a blender and whizz the mix until it all combines together (this takes a few minutes).

2 Mix in the orange zest.

3 Transfer to small bowls and sprinkle with the Super Duper Seed Mix (if using), then pop in the fridge to firm up for 20 minutes or so before serving. (It can be served straight away – it will just have a firmer texture if chilled.)

Serving ideas: Serve in the bowls or give baby a spoon of the mix – they don't need much as it's super rich!

Adaptations for the whole family: This is delicious as it is, but you could add a few raspberries to the top and a dollop of cream for real indulgence!

Switching ingredients in/out: Dairy-free Greek-style yoghurt works well in this too.

Storing leftovers/how to defrost: Without the seed mix, place into an airtight container in the fridge and eat within 2 days. Alternatively, place in the freezer and consume within 3 months. Defrost in the fridge overnight or until fully thawed.

Fruity Yoghurt Swirls

I always get a little frustrated by kids' yoghurts in the shops. Often manufacturers convince us that they are the best options for our little ones and, once they've had them and start to enjoy the sweetness of them, it's hard to go back to natural yoghurt. So I wanted to offer an alternative that adds a little sweetness naturally from the fruits, but isn't massively sweet. I *love* these combos, especially the pineapple and mango one. They are super easy, look fab with the coulis just swirled through and taste great! You can also use the coulis as a dip or mixed into other dishes to add a little extra flavour if you like.

Prep: 10 minutes
Makes: 3 bowls of coulis (each bowl serves 6–8 people)

For combo 1, Green:
2 ripe kiwis, peeled (about 130g)
80g green grapes (about 10–12)

For combo 2, Yellow:
100g ripe pineapple, cut into 2cm chunks (tinned works too)
100g mango, cut into 2cm chunks (frozen and slightly defrosted works too)

For combo 3, Red:
100g strawberries (about 5–6), hulled and halved
100g raspberries

natural yoghurt/dairy-free alternative, to serve

1 Whichever combo you are choosing, add those ingredients to a blender and whizz until combined.

2 You can either leave the coulis as it is for a thicker fruit puree or you can pass it through a sieve and strain into a bowl (this gives a stronger colour and a smoother texture).

3 Using around 2 tablespoons of coulis to 4 tablespoons of yoghurt (or dairy-free alternative), gently swirl the coulis through the yoghurt (not mixing completely), and serve. Delicious!

Storing leftovers/how to defrost: The coulis (without yoghurt) will keep in the fridge for 2 days in an airtight container or in the freezer for up to 3 months. (Pop the coulis into ice-cube trays and cover tightly before freezing.) Defrost in the fridge overnight.

Sweet Potato Nibbles

These fun little sweet potato nibbles will look brilliant with a party spread. They can easily be made vegan too, so everyone can enjoy them. Although a little fiddly, they are super tasty and make the nicest little snacks. I couldn't stop eating them when I first made them – I hope your little ones enjoy them too.

Prep: 10 minutes
Cook: 20 minutes
Makes: 30–35 nibbles

2 medium sweet potatoes (about 500g), sliced into 1cm rounds
1 tbsp olive oil
150g sour cream or dairy-free alternative
pincn of smoked paprika

For the topping:
1 ripe avocado, peeled and destoned
a squeeze of lemon or lime
50g tinned black beans, drained and rinsed (mashed for babies)
50g tinned sweetcorn, drained (mashed for babies)
¼ coloured pepper (about 30g), deseeded and very finely chopped
½ spring onion, trimmed and finely chopped (optional)

1   Preheat the oven to 210°C/190°C fan. Line a baking tray with greaseproof paper.

2   Pop the sweet potato slices onto the lined tray, drizzle with the oil and toss to make sure they are coated on each side. Bake for 20 minutes until golden and cooked through.

3   Meanwhile, make your toppings. Pop the avocado into a bowl and mash really well, then squeeze in a little lemon or lime juice.

4   In another bowl, add the black beans, sweetcorn, pepper and spring onion (if using) and mix to combine (or give it a pulse with a hand blender to chop it up slightly for little ones), then put to one side.

5   Once the potatoes are cooked, leave to cool a bit on the tray and then pop them onto a serving plate.

6   To assemble, add a little dollop of mashed avocado onto each sweet potato, then a teaspoon of the bean topping, then a little dollop of sour cream or dairy-free alternative.

7   To finish, dust with a little smoked paprika.

Adaptations for the whole family: You might like to sprinkle some hot paprika onto your portion before serving. For older kids, you can keep the bean/sweetcorn mix chunkier.

Storing leftovers/how to defrost: Cool the sweet potato to room temperature within 2 hours. Place into an airtight container in the fridge and eat within 2 days. Alternatively, place in the freezer with baking paper between and consume within 3 months. Defrost in the fridge overnight or until fully thawed. Reheat until piping hot and then allow to cool before serving. The bean topping can be stored in an airtight container in the fridge and consumed within 2 days or frozen and consumed within 3 months. Defrost in the fridge overnight.

Apple and Blackberry Crumble

I grew up with a dad who threw crumbles together from leftover produce all the time. We're a big crumble family and my two kids also love them. This one is even easier as you don't need to pre-cook the fruits, and yet it comes out super soft and delicious just the same. Apple and blackberry is a classic combination and this is a great one to make ahead and freeze for later. This recipe makes a double batch of the topping, so you're ahead for next time, so halve the topping ingredients if you don't want extra to save for another day.

Prep: 15–20 minutes
Cook: 40 minutes
Serves: 2 adults and 2 babies/toddlers, with leftovers

450g eating apples (about 3), peeled, cored and cut into thin wedges
150g fresh (or frozen) blackberries
zest and juice of 1 orange or clementine (or a good splash of fresh juice)

For the topping:
125g unsalted butter, cold and cubed, or plant-based spread
125g wholemeal or plain flour
100g porridge oats
1 tsp ground cinnamon

Adaptations for the whole family: Add a little demerara sugar to the top of your half if you like sweeter crumbles.

Tip: Throw in frozen apples or blackberries if you prefer.

1   Preheat the oven to 200°C/180°C fan.

2   Put the apples, blackberries and orange zest and juice into an ovenproof dish (about 24cm in diameter). Give it a mix around.

3   Pop into the oven for 10 minutes.

4   To make the topping, in a large bowl, add the butter and flour and rub it between your fingers and thumbs to create breadcrumbs, then add in the oats and cinnamon and give it a good mix.

5   Remove the crumble dish from the oven and carefully sprinkle half the topping on top of the fruit (save the rest for another time – see storage instructions below).

6   Bake for 30 minutes, or until golden and smelling delicious.

7   Leave to cool a little before serving. You can give the fruits a little mash if needed for young babies, but they are super soft in this recipe and easy to manage. The apple wedges are also easy for babies to have as finger foods too, so you could offer some of these on the side.

Serving ideas: Add a dollop of Greek yoghurt when serving if you like.

Switching ingredients in/out: Swap the apples and blackberries for roughly the same amounts of any fruits you fancy. Use plant-based spread or gluten-free flour if needed.

Storing leftovers/how to defrost: Will keep in the fridge for 2 days, covered or in an airtight container, or in the freezer for up to 3 months. (Pop the leftover topping into a bag and seal it airtight before freezing or freeze the whole crumble, covered.) Defrost in the fridge overnight, then reheat in the oven until piping hot. Allow to cool before serving.

Mango and Coconut Ice Cream

My kids both love mango and ice cream, so this was a no-brainer for me to create for this book. For younger babies, the cold might be a bit too much on their gums, so let it defrost a little before offering. Leave off the desiccated coconut for younger babies as this can be quite dry for them and a bit of a tricky texture to manage, but it's a lovely flavour addition for older kids and adults. This is such a simple and refreshing recipe that is super soft and creamy, and makes a fab party food option too.

Prep: 5 minutes
Chill time: 2 hours minimum
Serves: 6 people (adults and kids!)

500g frozen mango pieces
1 medium banana (about 100g), peeled and roughly broken into pieces
200ml tinned coconut milk, stirred well
2 tbsp desiccated coconut (optional)

1   Pop the mango and banana into a food processor. Pulse to combine (don't go crazy as you will whizz it again), then add in the coconut milk.

2   Whizz again until combined then pop into a dish (about 20 x 20cm), cover and leave in the freezer for a minimum of 2 hours to set a little.

3   If you're using the desiccated coconut, toast it in a dry frying pan over a medium heat for a few minutes (or until starting to colour lightly). Pour out into a bowl and leave to one side for serving.

4   To serve, leave the ice cream out for 10–15 minutes to soften a little, then scoop into bowls and sprinkle over the desiccated coconut (if using), or scoop into mini cones for older children and sprinkle with coconut.

Adaptations for the whole family: Drizzle your portion with some melted chocolate after scooping out.

Storing leftovers: Will keep in the freezer for up to 3 months.

Tip: Use up the leftover coconut milk in the Easy Chicken Satay recipe on page 149.

Mini Cinnamon Crunch Carrot Cakes

These little carrot cakes aren't super sweet, but with the icing they contain plenty of flavour and are great options for babies and toddlers. I love making these and having them with a cup of tea.

Prep: 10–15 minutes
Cook: 18–20 minutes
Makes: 10–12 cupcakes

1 large carrot (about 100g), peeled and coarsely grated
1 large banana (about 120g), peeled and mashed
1 large free-range egg or 1 flaxseed egg (see page 40)
2 tbsp apple juice or milk of choice
75ml olive oil
50g ground nuts, such as almonds, walnuts or pistachios (plus 1 tbsp for sprinkling over icing)
175g self-raising flour
½ tbsp ground cinnamon, plus extra to sprinkle

For the icing:
85g full-fat cream cheese or dairy-free alternative
2 tbsp thick Greek yoghurt
zest of ½ medium orange, plus 1–2 tsp juice

1   Preheat the oven to 200°C/180°C fan. Line a 12-hole cupcake or muffin tin with cases.

2   In a large bowl or stand mixer, mix the carrot, banana, egg or flaxseed egg, apple juice or milk and oil. Add in the nuts, flour and cinnamon, and give it a good mix, adding a splash more apple juice or milk if needed.

3   Divide the mix between the cupcake cases and bake for 18–20 minutes, or until golden, risen and cooked through.

4   Take the cupcakes out of the oven, leave to cool for 5 minutes then carefully remove to a cooling rack.

5   Meanwhile, make the icing. In a bowl, add the cream cheese, yoghurt and orange zest. Whisk together really well to create a smooth icing, then add in 1 teaspoon of orange juice and whisk, adding another if needed to loosen it a little.

6   Spread the icing over the top of the cooled cakes and sprinkle over the ground nuts and a little ground cinnamon to finish.

Adaptations for the whole family: Add a spoon or two of sugar into the mix for your portion if you want it a little sweeter – this works for older kids too.

Storing leftovers/how to defrost: Will keep in an airtight container in the fridge for 2 days or in the freezer for up to 3 months. Allow to thoroughly defrost in the fridge overnight before serving.

Afternoon Tea Scones and Jam

I love an afternoon tea with friends, so wanted to do a mini version for babies and toddlers. These scones are super easy to make and also really soft so are fine for babies who have tried a number of finger foods. You could add chopped/soaked raisins or other dried fruits for older children if you like. Additionally, you could fill them with cream cheese and a little thinly sliced cucumber too. You can use any frozen fruits to make the jam – it can be a little tart with berries alone (which we love in this house), but if you're looking for something sweeter, you could use some apple juice instead of water.

Prep: 15 minutes
Cook: 10–15 minutes
Makes: 10–12 scones

60g cold unsalted butter, cubed
300g self-raising flour, plus extra for dusting
160ml milk of choice, plus extra for glazing

For the chia seed jam:
250g frozen fruit
4 tsp chia seeds

For serving:
150g double cream, whipped, or Greek yoghurt or dairy-free alternative
strawberries, hulled and thinly sliced, to serve

Serving ideas: Serve alongside my Sweet Potato Twists (see page 75) and some sandwich fingers for a real afternoon tea experience.

1. Preheat the oven to 210°C/190°C fan. Line a large baking tray with greaseproof paper.

2. In a large bowl, add the butter and flour and rub it between your fingers and thumbs to create breadcrumbs.

3. Pour in the milk and mix, then bring the dough together into a ball with your hands. Transfer the dough onto a floured surface. Using a rolling pin, roll out the dough until it is 2cm thick. Using a 5–6cm cutter (or a small glass), cut out 10–12 scones. (You can reroll the pastry if you need to.)

4. Pop the scones onto the lined tray, then brush the tops with a little milk.

5. Bake for 10–15 minutes, or until cooked through and golden.

6. Meanwhile, make the chia seed jam. In a pan, add the fruit and 4 tablespoons of water and bring to the boil. Mash the fruit down, then mix in the chia seeds and cook for 5 minutes until thickened a little. Remove from the heat, then remove to a bowl to cool a little.

7. Once the scones are cooked, remove to a cooling rack to cool a little, then serve spread with the whipped cream or yoghurt and chia seed jam, with strawberry slices on top.

Storing leftovers/how to defrost: The scones will keep at room temperature in an airtight container for 2 days or in the freezer for 3 months. The jam will keep in a jar or airtight container in the fridge for 1 week or in the freezer for about 3 weeks. Remove both from the freezer and allow to thoroughly defrost in the fridge overnight before serving.

Baby's First Cheesecake

I'm a little obsessed with these mini cheesecakes! They are not sweet, as there is no added sugar in them, but they are very flavourful regardless, with the cinnamon and orange tang, and especially with some really ripe and delicious strawberries sliced on top. The base of these can be quite solid when cold, so if you're serving to a young baby, just let it warm a little at room temperature and it should be nice and crumbly for them. I hope you enjoy these!

Prep: 20 minutes
Makes: 12 cheesecakes

150g porridge oats
25g nuts (such as almonds and pistachios) and 25g seeds (such as sunflower seeds) or 50g of pre-ground nuts and seeds
100g unsalted butter or plant-based spread
2 tsp ground cinnamon
zest of 1 orange and juice of ½
165g full-fat cream cheese or dairy-free alternative
100g thick Greek yoghurt or dairy-free alternative
¼ tsp vanilla bean paste or vanilla extract (optional)
125g strawberries, hulled and thinly cut into vertical slices (optional)

1 Line a 12-hole cupcake or muffin tin with cases.

2 Add the oats, nuts and seeds to a blender and blitz to create a crumb texture.

3 Melt the butter in a medium saucepan. Remove from the heat and add the blitzed oats, nuts and seeds, cinnamon and orange zest. Give it a good mix, then divide it between the 12 muffin cases. Push it down really well using the back of a small spoon, then pop in the fridge while you make the filling.

4 In a bowl, mix together the cream cheese, yoghurt, orange juice and vanilla (if using). Take the biscuit bases out of the fridge, then carefully spread the filling over each biscuit base.

5 Top with the thinly sliced strawberries (if using), then pop back in the fridge for a minimum of 1 hour until you need them.

6 Peel off the cases and serve.

Adaptations for the whole family: These are really lovely as they are. Add a little extra fresh fruit, if you prefer it sweet, or drizzle on a little honey. For older children, add a few teaspoons of caster sugar to the biscuit base to add some sweetness.

Storing leftovers/how to defrost: Will keep in the fridge for 2 days in an airtight container or in the freezer for up to 3 months. Allow to thoroughly defrost in the fridge overnight before serving.

Measurement Conversions

Weights*

Metric	Imperial
15g	½oz
25g	1oz
40g	1½oz
50g	2oz
75g	3oz
100g	4oz
150g	5oz
175g	6oz
200g	7oz
225g	8oz
250g	9oz
275g	10oz
350g	12oz
375g	13oz
400g	14oz
425g	15oz
450g	1lb
550g	1¼lb
675g	1½lb
900g	2lb
1.5kg	3lb
1.75kg	4lb
2.25kg	5lb

*28.35g = 1oz but the measurements here have been rounded up or down to make conversion easier

Volume

Metric	Imperial
25ml	1 fluid ounce
50ml	2 fluid ounces
85ml	3 fluid ounces
150ml	5 fluid ounces (¼ pint)
300ml	10 fluid ounces (¼ pint)
450ml	15 fluid ounces (¾ pint)
600ml	1 pint
700ml	1¼ pints
900ml	1½ pints
1 litres	1¾ pints
1.2 litres	2 pints
1.25 litres	2¼ pints
1.5 litres	2½ pints
1.6 litres	2¾ pints
1.75 litres	3 pints
1.8 litres	3¼ pints
2 litres	3½ pints
2.1 litres	3¾ pints
2.25 litres	4 pints
2.75 litres	5 pints
3.4 litres	6 pints
3.9 litres	7 pints
5 litres	8 pints (1 gal)

Measurements

Metric	Imperial
0.5cm	¼ inch
1cm	½ inch
2.5cm	1 inch
5cm	2 inches
7.5cm	3 inches
10cm	4 inches
15cm	6 inches
18cm	7 inches
20cm	8 inches
23cm	9 inches
25cm	10 inches
30cm	12 inches

Oven Temperatures

140°C	275°F	Gas Mk 1
150°C	300°F	Gas Mk 2
160°C	325°F	Gas Mk 3
180°C	350°F	Gas Mk 4
190°C	375°F	Gas Mk 5
200°C	400°F	Gas Mk 6
220°C	425°F	Gas Mk 7
230°C	450°F	Gas Mk 8
240°C	475°F	Gas Mk 9

Further Resources

Allergy UK
Helpline: 01322 619898
Website: https://www.allergyuk.org

The British Society for Allergy & Clinical Immunology (BSACI)
Website: https://www.bsaci.org
Guide to preventing food allergy in your baby:
https://www.bsaci.org/wp-content/uploads/2020/02/pdf_Infant-feeding-and-allergy-prevention-PARENTS-FINAL-booklet.pdf

Charlotte Stirling-Reed
For more advice and information on feeding your child, as well as how to join my courses, please see my website or follow me on Instagram:
Website: https://www.srnutrition.co.uk
Instagram: sr_nutrition

My 'Online Weaning Course' includes everything you need to know in spoken, video format. It also has some recipes and note pages and multiple exclusive handouts.

My 'Fussy Eating Crash Course' helps you be ready for the food refusal stage. This course can help give you reassurance and tips and tricks about fussy eating.

All my previous books influenced this one and offer specific support at different times of your feeding journey with little ones:

How to Wean Your Baby (Vermilion, 2021)
How to Feed Your Toddler (Vermilion, 2022)
How to Feed Your Family (Vermilion, 2023)

Thank Yous

There are so many to dish out, it's hard to even begin.

The biggest thank you has to go to my two children, without whom I probably wouldn't be writing ANY of these books. I know I moan about you sometimes, but my goodness I love being your mummy! Thank you for being you and thank you for all the super honest feedback you (and your dad!) give me on my recipes on a daily basis. These books wouldn't be what they are without your input.

Thanks to my little team of recipe developers and testers – it's not an easy task planning, developing, testing and finessing 100 recipes, but we did it. So grateful to you both Christina Mackenzie and Emily Kerrigan. I think with us mums and foodies working on these recipes together, we've really cracked it and I'm so proud of them. Also a big shout out to all the friends and family who helped test, especially my dad and Laura Matthews who gave such incredible feedback every time – we all make a fab team.

The photographers Liz and Max and food stylist Frankie always produce the most incredible visuals for my book – I love having you as part of the team, as well as my incredible editor, Julia Kellaway – you make the book what it is! Also, thank you to the brilliant designer, Louise Evans.

Joe – I can't not say thank you to my friend Joe Wicks. Without him I simply wouldn't be where I am in my career today and I'm genuinely so, so grateful for this and for his continued guidance, advice and friendship. You're brilliant!

I'm so honoured to be published by Ebury – thank you for looking after me so well and always supporting me, even on the 325th edit 😉. A huge thank you to Sam Jackson and Leah Feltham and the whole marketing team! Lastly, thank you to my agents and team at Bev James Management, especially Liz, Izzy and Tom – your backing throughout has been indispensable.

About the Author

Charlotte Stirling-Reed is a leading nutritionist based in the UK and author of the bestsellers *How to Wean Your Baby*, *How to Feed Your Toddler* and *How to Feed Your Family*.

Charlotte began her working life in the NHS after gaining a first-class honours degree in Nutrition and Human Biology and then a postgraduate degree in Nutrition and Public Health. Charlotte now works with a variety of global brands and her expertise is highly sought after by the media and celebrities alike. She has appeared across major UK TV channels and radio stations and worked alongside Joe Wicks, AKA The Body Coach, on his book *Wean in 15*.

Charlotte supports thousands of families with evidence-based advice on feeding their babies, toddlers and young children through her popular Instagram platform (@SR_Nutrition). Charlotte's reassuring approach and easy, family-friendly recipes are informed by life with her own little foodies, Raffy and Ada.

Index

1

Vermilion, an imprint of Ebury Publishing
Penguin Random House UK
One Embassy Gardens, 8 Viaduct Gardens,
Nine Elms, London SW11 7BW

Vermilion is part of the Penguin Random House group of companies whose addresses
can be found at global.penguinrandomhouse.com

Penguin
Random House
UK

First published by Vermilion in 2025

www.penguin.co.uk

A CIP catalogue record for this book is available from the British Library

Commissioning Editor: Sam Jackson
Project Editor: Leah Feltham
Editor: Julia Kellaway
Recipe developer: Christina Mackenzie
Recipe testing: Emily Kerrigan
Designer & illustrator: Louise Evans
Photographer: Haarala Hamilton
Food & prop stylist: Frankie Unsworth
Stylist assistant: Georgia Rudd
Hair & make-up: Sara Clark

ISBN 9781785044830

Printed and bound in China by C & C Offset Printing Co., Ltd.

The authorised representative in the EEA is Penguin Random House Ireland,
Morrison Chambers, 32 Nassau Street, Dublin D02 YH68.

Penguin Random House is committed to a sustainable future for
our business, our readers and our planet. This book is made from
Forest Stewardship Council® certified paper.